The GIRO d'ITALIA

Coppi versus Bartali

at the 1949 Tour of Italy

ISBN: 1-884737-51-x

Printed in the U.S.A.

Library of Congress Cataloging-in-Publication Data Applied For.

VeloPress
1830 N 55th Street
Boulder, Colorado 80301-2700
USA

303/440-0601
303/444-6788 fax
e-mail: velopress@7dogs.com

To purchase additional copies of this book
or other Velo products,
Call 800/234-8356, or visit our
Web site at www.velogear.com

Cover photos: Fotocronache Olympia; Photosport International
Interior photos: Fotocronache Olympia
Photo collage/book design: Erin Johnson

table of contents

THE DUEL BETWEEN
COPPI AND BARTALI

ALF A CENTURY HAS PASSED SINCE THE FAMED ITALIAN WRITER and poet Dino Buzzati followed the 1949 Giro d'Italia—Italy's equivalent of the Tour de France. Buzzati had never seen a top-level bicycle race before, but he had of course heard of Italian cycling's then leading lights: Gino Bartali, the 34-year-old Tuscan, who had won the Giro three times before (1936, 1937 and 1946), and Fausto Coppi from Piedmont, four years younger, who won the Giro on his 1940 debut—when Bartali was his teammate—and again in 1947.

By 1949, four years after Italy's destruction in World War II, Coppi and Bartali were regarded as equals, and their rivalry consumed—and divided—the country. Buzzati focused on this rivalry in his daily dispatches from the Giro, comparing Coppi and Bartali with, respectively, Achilles and Hector, the mythological figures from Homer's "The Iliad."

The two heroes of the 1949 Giro fought their "fight to the death" in the French Alps, on the legendary seventeenth stage from Cuneo to Pinerolo over five giant mountain passes. Back then the roads through the mountains were gravel

1

or dirt—dusty in the dry, muddy in the wet. And that particular stage was 254 kilometers (158 miles) long, and on a wet, stormy day the best riders took almost ten hours to complete it.

There was no live television in those days, so fans would gather in local bars and cafés to listen to the brief reports of radio commentators. For the real story of the race, they would wait until the next morning and read the specialist sportswriters' reports in the daily newspapers. One can only imagine what was the impact on those who read Buzzati's sometimes outlandish, sometimes intellectual, sometimes melodramatic stories during that Giro of 1949.

Besides Homer, the Italian celebrity writer—his equivalent today would probably be American author Tom Wolfe—made many historical references. In the early "chapters," he compares the Giro riders' voyage from Genoa to the race start in Sicily with that made by Giuseppe Garibaldi, the popular 19th century Italian patriot, in 1859. In Sicily, Garibaldi's red-shirted "Thousand" became a twenty-thousand-strong army, which defeated the occupying forces, marched on Naples, and eventually facilitated Italy's unification.

Buzzati echoes the hero quality of Achilles and Garibaldi in his descriptions of the dramatic 1949 Giro. He takes great care in getting into the minds of both the two super-champions—whom he refers to as the giants, the aces or the *campionissimi*—and the team workers, the *gregari*. The other leading characters in this modern-day odyssey are the spectators, the great Italian public, to whom Buzzati makes constant references, including those who died in the town of Cassino, which saw a strategic battle in World War II between the U.S. and German forces.

But throughout the book, the strong thread of the Coppi-Bartali duel never wavers. Looking back, it is ironic that Coppi went on to live a tragic life that included the death of his brother Serse in a bike race, and his own death, from malaria, just after his fortieth birthday. In contrast, the aging rider who Buzzati likened to the tragic Hector, Bartali, has lived peacefully since his retirement, and except for a short hospitalization in 1998, looks set to see in the new millennium following his eighty-fifth birthday.

—*John Wilcockson*
December 1998

NOTE

This book is born of an idea of Claudio Marabini who gave a lecture entitled "Dino Buzzati at the Giro d'Italia" at the Buzzati Study Congress held in Venice, November 3-4, 1980, at the Cini Foundation. The title refers to a series of twenty-five reports that the writer from Belluno had published in the *Corriere della Sera* between May 18 and June 14, 1949, as a special correspondent assigned to the 32nd Giro d'Italia.

Three of Buzzati's articles are missing (those for three Mondays, this being the day that the *Corriere della Sera* is not published). We have included three reports by Ciro Verratti, correspondent for the *Corriere d'Informazione*, in order to enable the reader to revisit the Giro in its entirety. We are indebted to the Verratti heirs for their kind permission to use the reports.

The data relative to the order of arrivals at all stages and to daily classifications have been drawn either from the *Corriere della Sera* or the *Corriere d'Informazione.*

AUSTRIA

SWITZERLAND

Bolzano

Bassano

Udine

Milan
ARRIVO

Venice

FRANCE

Turin

Pinerolo
Cuneo

Modena

Genoa

YUGOSLAVIA

San Remo

Montecatini

ITALY

Pesaro

Adriatic Sea

🛥 **Pre-race itinerary**

🕐 **Time trial**

▲ **Gran Premio
della Montagna**

1 Colle del Contrasto
2 Tiriolo
3 Passo di Rolle
4 Passo Pordoi
5 Passo di Gardena
6 Abetone
7 Passo di Bracco
8 Passo di Nava
9 Col de Vars
10 Col de l Izoard
11 Col de Montgen vre
12 Madonna del Ghisallo

Rome

Naples

Salerno

Sardinia

Tyrrhenian
Sea

Cosenza

Villa San
Giovanni

Palermo
PARTENZA

Messina

Catania

Sicily

Mediterranean Sea

1

FOR THE "HARD WORKERS" OF THE ROAD, NIGHT ON THE OCEAN LINER

Aboard the "Saturnia," the night of May 17

WE OPEN THE DOOR TO CABIN No. 223, second tourist class. Darkness, and the musical whisper of a fan. In here are Lucien Buysse, Roger Missine, Jef Van der Helst, Giuseppe Cerami, racing cyclists. They are asleep.

We open the door to cabin No. 234. Darkness here, too. This one is assigned to Albert Dubuisson and Jean Lesage. They, too, are sleeping. And here and there, behind the white doors along the deserted corridor, the others, Kubler, Logli, Monari, Valenta, Conte, Crippa, et cetera. They are being borne through the Tyrrhenian night lulled by the subdued purr of the ship whose stupendous lights are seen even from a great distance by fishermen in their small boats, as if they were seeing a mirage, and though they know what it is, they point at, call out to one another hardly able to believe their eyes.

Buysse, Missine, Van der Helst, Cerami, et cetera. Names, some famous and some not. Tomorrow morning we land at Naples; in the evening we set sail on another ship. The day after tomorrow, the landing at Palermo. One more day, and then everybody will climb on their saddles, settle their feet on the pedals and, clenching their teeth, off they will gallop, ready for the great adventure. But tonight, in the brightly lit ship, how relaxed their dreams must be.

From Genoa, with this paradoxical maritime debut, the 32nd Giro d'Italia began, in fact, this morning. But only a small part of the Giro's protoganists is on board the Saturnia: team managers, technical directors, mechanics, masseurs, and so on…. As for actual cyclists, there are only 23. Coppi, for example, is not there, nor Bartali. Many of them, never having sailed, especially those from rural areas, blindly believed the fearful tales of seasickness and, right now, are in old trains going down the peninsula…. Many will join the navigators, leaving from Naples. But, historically, the story of the Giro rightly began this morning the moment the gangplank was withdrawn from the ship's side and the moorings cast off.

Should we now abstain from making such an instinctive comparison with the departure of the Mille di Quarto[1]? Too trite, perhaps? Not at all. We will absolutely not abstain from doing so neither now nor on any eventual future occasions, if they should present themselves. It would amount to betraying the truth. Because it is impossible that whoever invented this unprecedented start did so without remember-

---

1. Reference to Garibaldi's expedition, which left from Quarto, in Liguria, on May 6, 1860.

ing the Lion of Caprera[2]. And even admitting that none of the organizers had consciously thought about him, then it means that unwittingly they repeated for cycling, rather than for military purposes, Garibaldi's reasoning of 90 years ago. Is there perhaps a sort of peninsular strategy that recurs as an obligatory solution for whomever has decided to conquer Italy? And which does not allow a deviation from the traditional path even when the invasion is launched by bicycle?

However, tonight the heroes of the forthcoming adventure are not keeping watch as Garibaldi's sentries did on the maintops of the Piemonte and Lombardo[3]. The champions are sleeping, savoring the sweetness of this comfortable, elegant night, lulled by the hundred voices of the ship that in the wee hours tell wonderful stories about oceans, whales, skyscrapers, exotic lovers, distant cities with names too difficult to pronounce.

Tomorrow, at breakneck speed, they will tackle the road, the great enemy, straight and long, that ends in nothing on the horizon, or winding and steep like a crag, the very sight of which takes one's breath away, a road covered with stones, or dust, or mud, or tarmac, or deferred by potholes. The endless ribbon that must be swallowed little by little. But tonight there is only the immense, broad avenue of the sea that has no holes, nor curbs, nor climbs, a soft carpet, or so it seems, that the ship's prow cuts into with frightening ease as if it were made of silk, with no need for the calf muscles to push it with strokes of the pedal.

Tomorrow, there will be sweat, cramps, aching knees,

2. Caprera is the island near Sardinia where Garibaldi chose to retire at the end of his life.
3. Piemonte and Lombardo were the ships used by Garibaldi to take his troops to Sicily.

hearts in the throat, muscle fatigue, thirst, curses, flat tires, collapse of body and soul, that bitter taste in the mouth when the others, the good ones, break away, disappearing in a whirlwind of cheers. But tonight, lying in the soft berth, the soothed muscles relax: they are young, resilient, tonight extraordinary, irresistible, puffed up by the promise of victories.

Tomorrow, there will be the team manager's merciless orders, the need to drag the "captain" who will not feel up to it, haul him up the slopes like a sack, fruitlessly throwing away in the process the best of their own strength, on the very day when he, a *gregario*[4], was planning a solo attack. But tonight there are no orders from the team manager, no differences in status. Tonight, even the lowliest trainee is like a Napoleon. And he dreams.

He dreams, the little soldier of the roads, who has never heard the crowd roar his name, nor been lifted on to the shoulders of the delirious throng after his victory. He is dreaming of what all men at one time or another have an absolute need to imagine, otherwise life would be too hard to bear. He is dreaming of his Giro d'Italia...an awe-inspiring revenge. Right from the first stage, of course. At 106 kilometers from Palermo, where the road begins to climb rudely toward the Colle del Contrasto, more than 3000 feet above sea level, out of the thundering ranks of racers, still as compact as a herd of buffalo, who leaps out, no other than he, the *gregario*, the unknown one, whose name children have never chalked on suburban walls, neither to encourage him, nor denigrate him. Alone, he hurls himself like a madman up the steep ascent; and the others don't even pay any attention

4. Italian term for a team worker, or domestique.

to him. "What an idiot," says someone who knows it all, "just the best way to do yourself in; in five minutes at the most you will explode." But he continues to fly. As if carried by a supernatural impetus, he eats up switchback after switch-back as if, instead of climbing, he was hurtling down the Stelvio or some other mountain pass. The others, in the rear, are now no longer visible. People along the road shout bravo Bartali, but he shakes his head to make them understand that he is someone else. Who is he, then? No one recognizes him. In order to identify him, his number must be checked on the list printed in the newspaper. And panic runs through Sicily.

When will the wretch cut it out? The joke ends up irritating everybody. Now it is too much. Let's teach that madcap a lesson. The aces arch their backs. Yes, it is Coppi in person who will mete out the punishment. Bartali, of course, is stuck to Coppi's ribs. What had appeared to be an amusement turns into a gigantic battle. But he, the unknown one, the last of the last, has donned wings. A twenty-minute lead, twenty-five, thirty. Compared with him, who are the *campionissimi*? What are Fausto and Gino? Poor grubs, plodding in his wake, but far, far away, losing minute after minute.

Here is Catania, finally. The rumor of the miracle has traveled even more rapidly than he, and it has preceded him, unleashing a frenzy of crowds, flags, applause, flowers, kisses, brass bands. The time-keepers, eyes staring, scan the road on which he arrives unexpectedly like an arrow, a road that is clear, totally deserted, incredibly empty. And meanwhile, the watch hands run on, and still no one appears. Forty-seven minutes, forty-eight, fifty-five, sixty! One hour and five minutes go by before the pursuers are seen emerging in the distance.... And the crowd stays to look at them, in silence.

How easy it is to dream this night on board the great illuminated ship. But why be satisfied with one stage? Why not up the lead to a couple of hours? And why not extend the miracle to the very last finishing line? The average for the Giro: 44 kilometers per hour. A day-and-a-half's lead over the second. Coppi out of his mind, Bartali shut up in a monastery. After all, what does it cost? Lying back in his berth, he who will never finish in front, the "pen pusher" of the road, the faithful slave, the most humble of the humble, smiles, victorious, vindicated.

But perhaps it's not like that. It may be that even these fantasies are denied him; and even while he sleeps, he remains a poor *gregario*; that he is simply sleeping, perhaps, relaxed like a beast of burden, weary after the long road raced, exhausted by the distance still to be faced. Because he knows he has no hopes. So then, it is better simply to sleep. Sleep and nothing else. And that he dreams of nothing.

TWO NAMES FOLLOW THE CYCLISTS
DURING A TRAINING SESSION
ALONG THE GULF

Aboard the "Città di Tunisi," the night of May 18

SPARSE CROWD, REALLY SPARSE, TO TELL the truth, was waiting at the so-called gates (but the gates are no longer there) of the Naples harbor at 7:30 this morning. Youths in shabby clothes, others a little better dressed, a little old man, who was extremely well attired, a dozen street urchins (but are they still called *scugnizzi*?). There were also a couple of girls. What had got them out of bed at such an unlikely hour? Presumably, the arrival of the "Saturnia," since at that  moment the splendid ship was coming alongside, with solemnity, the Beverello wharf. But did they know who in particular was supposed to disembark? The youths, the old man, the *scugnizzi*, the two girls, still a bit sleepy, were making no move. And it is difficult in Naples to pigeon-hole people at first sight. Then it became clear they were there to welcome the Giro d'Italia racers. It became clear when the cyclists, after having disembarked, headed toward the vast square behind the wharf.

In the weak sun—it was a misty morning, with a dark cloud hanging over San Marino—the chrome on the bicycles sparkled with all their brilliance. Then we saw the characteristic jersey, blue for the most part. The champions were dressed for the race, as if the departure point of the Giro were there, a few steps away, in the piazza Municipio.

After leaving the vessel early in the morning, they could wait until evening to board the "Città di Tunisi," on which at this moment they are sailing toward Sicily. An entire day at their disposal. Twelve precious hours for the legs that on Saturday will be subjected to one of the most grueling contests conceived by man. Beware of starting off without having warmed up beforehand! A few days of inactivity are enough to make the muscles sluggish, even after conscientious training. The calves turn to wood. So this free day to stretch the legs comes as a blessing: a ride of one hundred, one hundred and fifty kilometers—or perhaps more—at thirty-five kilometers per hour, along the Gulf road, toward Sorrento and Amalfi.

The little crowd becomes restless. They are well-intentioned, even affectionate, but they lack the latest information. Bartali? they ask. And Coppi? Isn't Coppi here? Considering the confusion, it is easy to be mistaken, one has to admit. Even though he is a bit too tall, Crippa can be mistaken from a distance for the great champion from Castellania. Supporting the apocryphal identification is the little old man, who stubbornly winks joyfully at his presumed idol, while waving his cane in the air. But the racers move on, trying to get out of the enthusiastic mob without making a fuss. It's not that they give themselves airs. That's just the way they are: serious and, in a way, preoccupied. Perhaps they expected more? They pass through the crush, their attitude detached and indifferent, which is the best way to excite even more the curiosity and submission of the *tifosi*.[5] "Long live Gino!" someone shouts. Applause responds here and there. But the racers continue on, holding up their shiny bicycles, so slender and light. They do not smile, nor are they overly friendly. Perhaps they have been hurt by the hurrahs for Coppi and Bartali, without actually realizing it. Those hurrahs serve as a reminder of the differences. And they, the *gregari*, the still unknown young ones—the Monaris, the Nanninis, the Marangonis, the Brignoles, the Bensos—know only too well that differences exist. Naturally, it is easy to fool oneself, but there is also a limit: stopwatches and order of arrivals speak clearly enough. The differences do exist. But is it necessary to be reminded? Coppi is not here, he will come down by train. Nor did Bartali take the ship. Haven't you yet seen that your favorites are not here?

However, the *tifosi* are kind, in a sense extremely kind; they are easily satisfied. In the absence of the biggest guns, the secondary riders will do, even those of small caliber suffice. Enthusiasts are not fussy. When they finally understand that the two supreme giants are not present, they still welcome the other cyclists just as warmly. "Bravo Cerami!" One of the few well-informed fans shouts, refering to the most brilliant member of the Ganna team. He recognized him

5. *Tifosi* is the Italian word for "sports fans."

thanks to a photo in the newspaper. But Cerami is a Belgian Italian: his name is pronounced Seramì, so he is unaware that they called after him. "Bravo Kublerre!" yells another kind-hearted fan. Perhaps he's a fan of the Swiss cyclist Kubler? By no means! But he found out that Kubler was on the "Saturnia"; the name was more or less familiar to him, so he thought it would be nice to welcome him. The enthusiasm stored up for the two great ones has to be expended somehow, one can't just take it back home after getting up so early. "Bravo Kublerre," then. But Kubler isn't here either, at the last minute he decided not to board, he will go to Palermo by train; and even if he were here, he probably wouldn't turn around, hearing his name pronounced so badly.

Finally extricating themselves from the crowd, the racers get ready to leave. Everybody crowds around them. "No, no",—would like to say the *scugnizzi*, the youths in shabby clothes and those better dressed, the two girls (only the little old man has gone, disappointed, twirling his cane, disdainfully)—"it is really you who we are welcoming." Not Bartali; not Coppi, but you. If we shouted Bartali and Coppi, we were motivated only by etiquette, but we couldn't care less about them. It is really you we love, you, the young men of the future. You, Conti, you also, Crippa, and you just the same, Cerami, who everybody says is gifted, even if your name is pronounced the French way. After all, aren't they heroes, too? The applause, by tacit consent, grows louder and heartier. There is even someone who exaggerates: "Down with Bartali," he shouts, hoping it will be appreciated.

But the racers remain withdrawn, silent and serious, almost sullen, as if brooding over a mysterious insult. They slip their right foot into the toe clip, also lifting the left foot from the ground, and they take off, bending themselves over, ungainly, across the piazza Municipale. They are already at the corner of via De Prettis, now they have disappeared. Then the *tifosi* breaks up at last, they are embarrassed, assume an air of uneasiness, light cigarettes, yawn. It was only by chance that they were there.

Meanwhile, the racers ride farther away. The Rettifilo [one of the broad avenues of Naples] is already behind them. They pedal with fury on the road to Castellamare. Several windows are flung open. The silhouettes of several boys are seen flying out of the doors and rushing to the edge of the road. They get there too late, when the group, and its sonorous metallic rustling is already far away. Yet in their wake the cyclists hear shouts, ever louder, pursuing them. They are formless voices, shouts, nothing else. But two vowels are constantly repeated, always the same haunting vowels: "Aaah! Oooh! Bartali! Coppi!"

That's what the impromptu *tifosi* throw out; and they are just guessing. Angry, the cyclists pedal, at forty, forty-one kilometers an hour, tearing away to free themselves from the unpleasant sounds. Uselessly. The harder they go, the more sudden are the shouts that pursue them, the misunderstanding easier and more frequent. "Aaah! Ooooh!" Nothing else, like a tireless, malignant echo. The sun is already high, it's hot. Bent over by their efforts, their faces set hard and burning, the young champions continue their headlong flight. From the fields, from the dark doors of the houses, from the ditches, always the same damned two sounds. Other people's fame. And what about theirs?

3

TO RACE? IT'S WONDERFUL

Palermo, the night of May 19

UE TO A SET OF CIRCUMSTANCES THAT ARE probably linked to the whims of fate and about which it is now too late to complain, he who today writes this article as a reporter assigned to follow the Giro d'Italia has never seen a bicycle road race.

Races, he who writes these lines has certainly seen, on water and on land, in one form or another; never, however, has he seen the greats of bike racing competing under the sun, each with a number stuck on his back, spare tires slung over their shoulders, his face chalky with dust. He has seen, for example, children running to school when they were late, lightning darting across the sky during a storm, people rushing toward air-raid shelters as sirens blared. Once I even saw a thief running, practically flying, being chased down the via Andrea del Sarto in Milan; and then they caught up with him and beat him; but I couldn't guarantee it because it all happened at the end of the street and there was a lot of confusion. I have seen ostriches run with the speed of gunshots in the African desert; I have seen shells, with their little red lights, launched from enemy ships, race across the night sky, inscribing delicate, fascinating curves, and some of them actually bounced on the water just like a puck, crazily splashing far away. I have seen fast trains in the approaching dusk, with their small windows already illuminated, and the dreams and fantasies they arouse as they hurtled across the deserted countryside; they were splendid.

On the via Aurelia, many years ago, I saw a jersey-clad racer training and someone said it was Girardango, but I don't think so because it didn't look like him. I have also seen Charles the Bold's courier crawling through the forest, bringing a last-minute pardon to his faithful squire who was falsely accused of treason and whose blond head the executioner was about to chop off; but all this was happening in a movie and perhaps it wasn't all true. I have seen with my own eyes, just before dawn, a couple of flying saucers hovering over the rooftops of Milan; they were red and appeared to be friendly; nevertheless, nobody wanted to believe me. I have seen time fly—alas, so many years, months and days—as it plays havoc with we humans, changing our faces little by little; and its frightening speed that, I assume, even though it is not timed, is much faster than any average speed reached by racing cyclists, car racers, aviators or astronauts from time immemorial. Me, too; after all, when I was a boy, I raced astride a bicycle whose mudguards I had removed so it would look a little like the ones the champions used; and I remember that one evening I stuck close to Alfonsina Strada's wheel for two whole laps around the Park, I swear it, after which I exploded, leaving me humiliated; especially as, after she had shot off like an arrow, I was grabbed by a policeman and fined twenty lire (for speeding: at that time it amounted to an enormous sum of money). I have seen quite a number of things race, then, never, however, the giants of the road facing each other in a regular race sanctioned by cycling's top organizations. And this, no doubt, is certainly a drawback for a reporter who is getting ready to record an epic such as cycling's Giro d'Italia.

It is this deficiency that my fellow travelers, veterans of the Giro, take advantage of, I don't know whether out of kindness or malice. And since the Giro, in a certain sense, already began the day before yesterday in Genoa, from where a part of the caravan and the cyclists reached Naples by sea, and then Palermo (an odd news item: yesterday evening, off the coast of Capri, Serse Coppi had to suddenly lie down in his berth because he started to feel seasick, and even his brother Fausto did not appear to be completely at ease, even though the "Città di Tunisi" seemed as motionless as a massive basalt cliff); for this reason, in short, there was plenty of time for these old hands, fountains of knowledge, to educate me, continually exchanging references, humiliating for me…do you remember?…Camusso punctured on the Ghisallo[6], and Pellisier started an all-out fight with Antonin Magne at the finishing line. There were those who terrorized me, and others who gave me a glimpse of the nineteen stages as a series of restful heavens. They told me so many stories that, whatever the case, whether the Giro turns out

6. Madonna del Ghisallo is a mountain pass north of Milan.

to be a costumed kermesse or a torture or a gigantic affair of a lyric poem or a comedy or a savage war, at least one of them, the veterans who lecture me, will be right.

One of them says that the Giro is a wonderful physical tonic, and extraordinary outing in the country, a pilgrimage from one trattoria to another through gastronomic Italy. At one time, he says that he used to go every year to Montecatini; now, instead, he follows the Giro and benefits far more from it. When he gets back home, he tells us, his wife is amazed at how much younger he looks.

Another one, with equal experience and seniority, instead maintains that the Giro is an infernal machine designed to destroy men, racers, helpers, officials, journalists, photographers, et cetera. He says that for three weeks you fast, or almost, eating at most a heavy sandwich at breakfast, and in the evening a meal that is choked down because you are in a hurry and exhausted. As for sleep, he adds, that's even worse. Last year, for example, he affirms, he managed to sleep four hours in a row only between stages, and he got a complete night's sleep only after the last finishing line. But can that be true?

One fellow tells me it's all a set-up. The cyclists arrive first, second and third, and so on, on the basis of pre-arranged plots, corruption, obscure higher interests. He is probably a believer in dialectical materialism that explains everything with so-called economic factors, even Malabrocca's boils. Nonetheless, it is stimulating. The crowds are naïve, he says, and the fans who rave and lose sleep at night if their favorite has lost a couple of minutes are insane. The favorite probably had his own reasons, they can be sure.

But there is also the other fellow, no less shrewd and intelligent, who swears to the sublime purity of the Giro. He sees in it one of the last great phenomena of individual and collective mysticism. Even if they have loads of money, the racers are knocking themselves out just for the Idea. And it is the Idea, nothing less, that draws crowds to the sides of the road. Him, he repudiates everything: money, special interests, even the muscles. It is the Spirit, he says, only the power of the Spirit, that turns the wheels, climbs the Falzarego or the Pordoi mountains, and breaks records. In his opinion, the champions are Chosen heroes, the organizers priestly celebrants, and the anonymous sports fans a tide of burning faith.

There is yet another who complains all day long, cursing his decision to accept the assignment to the Giro again. He already anticipates dreadful strains, downpours, discomfort and bedbugs in the hotels, and colds. He swears that since a certain racer is absent, the race doesn't have the least interest for him and that it might as well not have been held, and that people don't give a hoot. In his worst moments, he even guarantees that bicycle racing is dead, dead and buried, that the champion breed has vanished, that in the atomic age the pedal crank is scrap metal belonging in a museum, and that to obstinately keep this shoddy affair going is ridiculous. But I look at him. He is about forty-five years old, robust, and always seems about to fend off a surprise attack; his face is a bit rough, stern, but likeable. I have been observing him closely for a day. I haven't figured out if he is a team manager or sports director of one of the teams, a head mechnic or masseur. He grumbles, sneers, looks on the dark side of everything, rushes from one spot to another breathlessly, as if a catastrophe were always about to happen. He sweats, curses, and smokes until late at night. He will stay this way, I assume, until the end of the Giro. A misfit, one might think at first glance, a person obliged to work unwillingly in an atmosphere that is hateful to him. So it seemed on first meeting him. But then, I changed my mind. I observe him now, as he gripes and dashes around acting like a sulky bulldog, I watch him with great pleasure and ask myself: How long has it been since I have seen anyone so happy?

4

A HUNDRED RACERS LEAVE
AT TOP SPEED ALONG THE ROAD
TAKEN BY GARIBALDI

Palermo, the night of May 20

EVERYTHING IS READY. IN A FEW HOURS, REVEILLE. The moment to leave has come. After the festivities, the bell-ringing, the songs, the flags, the emotional cheering of these two days, Palermo is sleeping with one eye open.

The bicycles are ready, shining like noble steeds on the eve of the tournament. The pink number plate is officially sealed to the frame. The lubricant has reached all the right spots. The tires, so narrow, are as smooth and taut as young snakes. The bolts have been tightened, the saddle tilted to the precise angle; and the height of the handlebars has been calculated to the millimeter. The bicycles have been good students; one could say they have learned all there is to learn, by now they know it by heart, after so many trials, tests, countertests. Is it possible for them to forget even a comma during the exam?

Ready, too, are the teams' secret tactical plans, worked on to the point of wearing out nerves and brains. There is no hypothesis, setback, surprise, or trap sprung by bad luck that has not been foreseen: whether it will rain, whether it will not rain, whether the aces will attack in force right away, or whether they will slack off, whether a *gregario* will break away, whether it will be dusty, whether it will be hot or cold, and so on. Whole volumes of bicycle racing knowledge are condensed in these mysterious strategies. The battlefield is new, at least in part. Several aspects of the regulations are of an audacious newness: such as intermediate sprints and the time bonuses at mountaintops. All this required the general staffs to weigh pros and cons, heed intuition, carry out unprecedented inspired studies. From the general to the colonel, down to the lowliest soldier, the password circulated with the maximum prudence. Will the soldiers honor it?

The soldiers are ready: one hundred and two racers (heroes, perhaps, tomorrow, or defeated infantrymen in shameful flight?). One more night and then no more daydreaming. Beginning tomorrow their sleep will be deep, compact and pitch black, so they can accumulate as much rest as possible, without the tiniest crack through which the deceptive light of dreams can penetrate. They are prepared. Their muscles have attained the needed elasticity. The prescribed hundreds of calories have gone down their alimentary canal. Their heartbeat has stabilized at the rhythm the doctors indicated. Each one has ready the rectangle of oilcloth with his racing number on it and the pins for attaching it to his back. Each one has ready his little secret weapons the others are not to know about: the charm with his children's pictures inside; the medal of his favorite Madonna; the ancient racing cap, all greasy, but unbeatable as a good luck charm; the special cycling shoes with the heels shaped a certain way, the same ones he wore three years ago for a resounding victory. With less imagination, one racer has slipped a little tube of amphetamine sulphate into the pocket of his jersey, another has an invigorating infusion specially created for him by the town pharmacist.

Food bags? The director of each team has already prepared them with paternal care, adapting the kind and quantity of food suitable to the taste and physique of each racer; one gets tenderloin, another boiled chicken, almost all of them get sugar cubes, butter and jam sandwiches, rice cakes, stewed fruit. Also ready is the masseur's equipment: band-aids, ointments, liniments, irrigations, laxatives, lightning-fast tonics. And then, the pep pills, the dynamic concoctions capable of making a corpse jump out of the casket like an acrobat.

Ready: the small bottles full of tea, coffee, mineral water. Ready: the spare parts. Ready: the publicity trucks that will transform the army of racers into an exciting carnival procession. Ready (set for five o'clock): the hands of the alarm clocks to wake up the fans in Palermo in time for tomorrow morning (those not yet worn out by today's exertions, the screaming, the crowds, the uproar, the frenzy, in front of the railings at the Politeama theatre, to watch the riders receiving their race numbers). Ready (at Catania, the first stage finish): the slogans written in praise of Cerami (pronounced Seramì), captain of the Belgian team, who was born in Catania. Ready: the flowers for Corrieri, the pride of Sicilian cycling. Ready: the circulars issued by the chief of police regarding public order along the route. Ready: the banners at the finishing lines, the triumphal arches, the garlands, the bands with their brass instruments shining like so many mirrors. Ready: the reporters' pencils, the cameras, the microphones. Ready: the yellow kerchief that our correspondent Di Francesco will wave as a sign of recognition when the caravan goes by, entering Cefalù, opposite the gas station.

But also ready is the enemy: stronger and more alarming this time than in all the years past. Beware, giants of the road, be on your guard. Sure, Palermo has embraced you as if you were her sons, these last two days. You have been showered with applause, festivities, smiles from beautiful girls. Just behind that, however, comes the bitterness. You will have to do battle with a proud, tenacious army right from the first day; and then, the day after tomorrow and the following day and always you will find it on the road. It will launch against you its regiments that have sinister names: they are called "kilometers," "clouds," and "thunder" (there is already a threatening mass in the sky), "dust," "climbs," "sirocco" (a hot, dry wind), "potholes," "muscle fatigue."

They will unload ice-cold showers on your back; wear you out with murderous ups and downs; throw treacherous fine gravel under your wheels. And then there is the infamous flat tire, the collision, the fall, the cramps, the boils, the thirst, the lumbago, not to speak of discouragement, and the solitude. There is also among the enemy's forbidden weapons the accursed and stinging penalty, which dissolves hours and hours of heroic exertion into nothing. So it will be, to the very end.

Who will hold out, oh gallant Garibaldians without bayonets? Who will become your Garibaldi? You don't have any generals yet; until now, you are simple soldiers. Stripes will have to be won. You begin all over again tomorrow morning. Victory, with its inscrutable visage, smiles indiscriminately on everyone.

Among you there are formidable warriors. When leaving for a new war, great hopes can fill even the most humble heart. One never knows. Those who in the past were covered with glory can be beaten at the first encounter. And those who remained little known behind the lines will perhaps leap to the front like an eagle. And then there are the new recruits, the unknown boys, to whom fate has perhaps already given the nod. Everything, really, starts over again; all the cards are still covered and hope flutters with equal intensity and impartiality over the starters.

Will the great endeavor be reduced to a duel between the sport's two giants, the two legendary aces? Or will a new name, destined to criss-cross the world, emerge unexpectedly from the ranks of the youngsters? Old Pavesi, discoverer of champions, diviner of future glory, the Nestor[7] of the Giro, has a slight, diplomatic grimace on his good-naturedly Mephistophelian face. Perhaps he has glimpsed, among so many yet unknown youngsters, someone marked by fate? Is the one destined to extinguish Bartali's and Coppi's light here among us? But old Pavesi smiles without saying yes or no. "We shall see," he replies. "Tomorrow, we shall see."

7. Nestor was the legendary king of Pylos in Messina, son of Nelly and Chloris. He was depicted in "The Iliad" as the oldest and wisest of the Greek chiefs, giving his counsel in long discourses.

The prologue has come to an end. We turn to the first page of the novel. We see a long road under the sun, flanked on one side and the other by a line of delirious humanity; and in the background, barely visible, a small, dark thing moving forward. God, how it is flying! It is a man on a bicycle, his head lowered, alone, racing madly toward the victory. Who is it? Who is it? A booming sound from down there is coming closer, and the roar of the crowd is like a thunderclap. Who is it? But we don't know how to reply. He is still too far away.

5

FAZIO KEPT HIS APPOINTMENT
WITH MAMMA

Catania, the night of May 21

BREAKAWAY. THE PRANK STARTED AS SOON AS we left Palermo. The crowd was still there on the roadsides, roaring. The sun. The small houses. From behind the curtains, still permeated with recent slumber, the uncomprehending faces of tousled young women appeared. Was that the race already? No, more likely a parade, a show, a triumphant procession as befits a departing army. Amid the roars, the one hundred and two bicycles passed by like a solid, metallic whine, and  when touched by the hum, the people shivered. The sun, still low in the sky, distorted and lengthened the shadows of the racers: there is Coppi's profile, and Leoni's, there is Bartali's Michelangelesque nose reflected on the white plaster walls. It looked like the day would be splendid. But what are those three dark, bagpipe-shaped clouds doing, poised over Monte

Pellegrino?

On these occasions, there is always somebody who fools around, almost as if hinting at something that could happen at the right time and place, when things get serious: like a child who threatens with his innocuous toy gun and says: "Bang!" Sometimes, however, and we don't know how, the innocuous little gun really goes off. Of the 4070 kilometers to race, still to come were 4068, to be exact, when the four riders broke away: Bof, Servadei, Lugatti and Monari. Oh, certainly, nothing to worry about. They were the first to admit it, including the bold Servadei, in whose knees years of stiffness has accumulated. Ready to be caught, in fact swallowed up by the main group, as it is customary to say; and then they smile, in case the giants look daggers at them, as if to say: "You didn't get angry, did you? If you deprive us of a little innocent satisfaction, what do we have left?"

It was right then that Mario Fazio, thirty years old, originally from Catania, now living in Brescia (a classic Sicilian face, dark-complexioned, thin, full lips) yielded to temptation. Maybe he had never before given it a thought, or, if he had, preferred not to dwell on the idea. However, Catania was the finishing line of the first stage and this meant a lot to him. Is it possible? he asked himself. And his response was: Let's risk it. He took the risk, shooting out of the group, which didn't pay him the slightest attention; it may be he was shielded by the infernal retinue of motorcycles and cars that in an attempt to keep an eye on everything create a frenzied merry-go-round with horns, sirens, klaxons, whistling, and so the race, from beginning to end, becomes a frenetic free-for-all, as though the bandit Giuliano had opened fire. Perhaps this did it. And, stuck to Fazio like glue, Biagioni slipped out behind him. Come on, let's go after the four who sprinted off as a prank, there they are, way down there rounding the curve. Then, two others took up the chase a few minutes later: Bevilacqua and Correa. Now, there were eight of them, set on taking a foolish risk: In front of them were the mountains, nothing but mountains, valleys and hills all the way to the end, and behind them the great champions, those whose pulse is forty at the top of the Stelvio, as if they had just awoken from a long nap.

It is wonderful to feel fresh and young on a Sicilian morning (you, too, Servadei right?), surrounded by the green countryside, and down below, the vast, deserted sea, without even a tiny boat on it, the rugged cliffs plunging steeply into the water and resembling gigantic primeval bastions. Forty-two, forty-three an hour, how long will they be able to keep it up? And their faces that a few minutes before, in Palermo, were so boyish, smooth, without a wrinkle, have changed into grotesque masks; one could say they were made of wax; now, in the heat, it's melting down in flaccid folds.

This is the man who feels locked into his horrendous exertion as if it were a prison: the world no longer exists, houses, men and women become unreal, like the rock climber, hanging on a vertical wall sees below him a few hundred meters from the small hotel the red cars, the tennis courts on which tiny white figures are moving, all that easy, serene life, and he is no longer able to believe in it, so absorbed is he by the abyss. So it is in the race. And little by little, everything around Fazio becomes shadowy. Vague, shapeless images flowing by on each side of him; shadows of the carts, the olive trees, the carabinieri with their machine guns, the black seminarians running down, down, panting, in search of Bartali. But Bartali is not there. It's then, the eight, that are there, isn't that enough? Perhaps it's because the sound of their names is not nice enough: Bartali, Bartali, the seminarians scream, their voices strident. Don't they have anything else to say, the morons?

A toe strap started to hurt. "I tightened it too much," Fazio thought, "but if I stop I'll be done for. It's hot. Couldn't these beastly cars stop passing. And why are they honking? Downhill toward the valleys at breakneck speed, you can make a good run for it, be careful, there is a bit of gravel on the asphalt. Now I can take a breather. It's your turn, Lugatti, to keep up the pace. And is this climb very long? No, thank goodness. Two hundred meters ahead, the reflection of the sun is already visible. Damn, now the saddle is beginning to hurt, too. It's new, I should have guessed it would hurt. (But will mamma be at the stadium in Catania?)" The runaways are dancing on their pedals, surprised by a new slope. They arch their backs, loosen their bodies the way giraffes do. They swing their heads comically, seen from behind they look as though they are saying no. No, no, in a sort of desperate anger directed against an invisible heckler who is moving back in front of them and never lets them catch up with him.

The fantastic Rock of Cefalù? The famous cathedral, "magnificent Norman-style temple begun by King Ruggero in 1131," et cetera? What do they matter today, the cathedrals, the sea, the landscape, even if they are among the most impressive in the world? Only the road exists, and nothing else; the road goes up, steep and rough and unyielding. The good part is now beginning. We are below the Colle del

Contrasto, with its King of the Mountains sprint line and its one-minute time bonus. One thousand, one hundred meters to climb. What is being thrown at them now? Rose petals, that's what. To hell with the roses, too. The others, the great champions, where are they, rather? That's what is important. Have they finally condescended to give battle? The sun has suddenly disappeared, gone is the festive atmosphere that permeated the landscape. Clouds, wind, chilly mountain air. And Bartali, where is he? Seven minutes back, a motorcyclist yells. But can we believe it?

Servadei, where have you gone, Servadei? Even looking back, he is no longer to be seen. Exploded? Bof gives up, too. It is cold. Right now, they are alone, alone on the threatening mountain. After passing through Mistretta, there is nothing along the sides of the road, just grass. Grass, and in the distance, flocks of sheep, with once in a while a shepherd, looking like someone out of a fable, laughing out loud like children do, not even knowing why. Biagioni, Bevilacqua, is it too difficult for you, too? They have been dropped. On the Contrasto's last steep slopes, it is finally Monari's turn to set the pace.

Is it over after that hump, up there, that it will end? Yes, God willing. A big red banner with "Finishing line" written on it trembles in the wind. Two young shepherds standing on the crags hold it suspended over the road. Fazio shoots ahead furiously. Monari, who thought he already had it made, sees him, sideways, charge by at an angle on his right like a stampeding buffalo. What is going on between those two? Was there a dirty move? Monari tries to clout Fazio. And, in order, they cross the summit: Fazio, Monari, Carrea. They immediately race down the descent, while right behind them, the cars pour in like a mad horde, their tires howling and screeching on the curves, on the edge of the precipice. The cold, a black sky, the first raindrops from a storm form little round spots in the dust.

And the giants? The giants arrive. The road is still long, the remaining mountains are smaller, but so numerous one gets tired counting them. Oh, no doubt, they'll get exhausted, the little finches, before reaching Catania. The giants take their work seriously, and the great strength of the massive peloton seems to multiply their fervor. They inspire fear when they hurtle through the hairpin bends, faster than skiers racing vertically down a wide, white piste. Doesn't that kind of punishment melt the wheel hubs? Don't the tires burn up? The earth's vertiginous gravity is not enough. Furiously, with all their strength, the racers attack. Their passage at 80 kilometers an hour generates a dull whistle.

Mountains, when will you end? Fazio and Carrca have remained alone, but the time has come to tackle the flats: In this low country, everything has to be paid for, even the solitary defiance of two men against a hundred has its cruel price. Thighs become leaden, burning sand has penetrated the knee joints, pedals feel as though they are bogged down in heavy mud, so stiff are they. (Will mamma come to the stadium? She had told him she would. His brothers, too? What will they say when they don't see him arrive? And, right now, where are they? Will they have finished eating, are they already on their way?) Alas, looking behind him, Fazio can see the other side of the valley, still far away, it's true, a long glitter of metal slipping down to the foot of the mountain. My god, how fast it is moving! Over there is Coppi; over there is

Ronconi; over there is Bartali, with his visor turned up, leading the group, pedaling with authority, stern and vengeful, as if he were on the way to inflict punishment.

Sweat is pouring down Carrea's vaguely Dantesque face; he, too, feels that his legs have turned to stone. And there is the last climb, the one leading to Adrano. Suddenly, the two racers appear to have stopped, so slowly are they moving. And behind them, like a pack of wolves, surge the Giro's great ones in a solid, irresistible mass. It is over.

So much is it over that the first of the pursuers reaches them. It is Cottur, in a flaming red jersey, driven by an obstinate and, today, marvelous youthfulness. "Fazio!" yells the good-natured fellow who resembles Dante, as if he were passing on an odd bit of news, "Go on! Go on! Fazio!" and he taps him on the shoulder. Then, suddenly, a miracle. The fiery agony that was burning him, having reached the utmost limit after which the heart explodes, disappears. A new, fresh flood of energy seeps into his muscles, loosens the iron knots gripping his legs, frees the wheels of their shackles. With just a few thrusts of the pedal, when the rumble of the motors was already closing in, announcing the arrival of the army, the two racers take off, flying again, as they did at the gates of Palermo. Their faces became dehumanized, swollen and dripping with perspiration, it's true, yet here they are charging like a train.

Catania is down there. At last the clouds open up. Rays of sunlight rain down on the countryside, on the lava flows, casting a radiant glow on the garlands, the motorcyclists' blue overalls, the ingenuous feminine laughter at the side of the road. Come on, you're beaten, Coppi, at this point you won't catch up with me. More towns, olive trees, carts, carabinieri, seminarians searching for Bartali unfurl once more, but they are festive images.

As he entered the stadium, the cheers of the crowd pouring over him, Fazio's eyes were seeking one thing. She was there. Right there, level with the finishing line, behind the wire fencing: mamma's face, plump, soothing, full of kindness, tranquility and laughter. It lasted just an instant because the last lap and the final sprint were still to be completed. Yet he caught sight of her; even if the crowd had been a hundred times larger, he would have discovered her just the same. Never had he seen her cry and laugh at the same time like that.

HUBBUB FROM THE GRANDSTANDS,
ALL AROUND MOUNT ETNA

Messina, the morning of May 22

ON ANTONIO PIZZOLARI, AN ELDERLY WELL-to-do gentleman, well known fifteen years ago by the nickname of "Il Bel Antonio"[8] (so radiant was his face and so many were the women who vainly threw themselves on their knees in front of him, moaning with love), lazily turned over between the bed-sheets in his elegant house in Catania, at— for Sicilians—the outrageously late hour of half past ten: "What now, people no longer have the right to sleep in Catania? What kind of infernal row is going on?" (In the room that is already lit up by the luminous reflections pouring in abundantly through the slats of the Persian blinds, he heads in his paja-mas toward the window. From between the slits in the shut-ters he squints at the crowd below that is making this

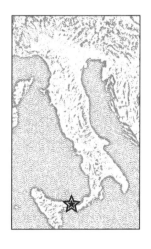

---

8. Allusion to "Il Bel Antonio," a novel by Vitaliano Brancati.

racket, yelling out names unknown to him. At the sight of an imposing cluster of people surrounding a young man in a blue jersey holding on to a bicycle, at this nauseating sight, he draws back, wiping a hand over his forehead and closes the inside shutters, plunging the room into darkness. He huddles down in bed again, buries his still handsome face in the pillows and falls asleep.)

A small boy, arriving out of breath in the piazza Palestro di Catania at 11:35: "Where is the starting point? What? They've already left? (How maddening!) How come? They've now begun to take off exactly on time?"

A goat, grazing among the lava flows near Misterbianco, addresses another goat: "You make me laugh, go on with you Coppi. You'll see if Bartali doesn't put him in his place on the climb up Mount Etna."

Rosì Capuana, eighteen years old, appearing at a window on the main street of Paternò (talking to herself): "So let's do this: If the first one to pass is wearing a blue jersey, it means that Carlo will show up tonight; if not, it means he has already left."

Giuseppe Ambrosini, the merciless race director, standing up in his car, his face scarlet, frantically waving a red flag, turning toward a car full of journalists that is trying to get through in the middle of this frightening flood of racers, cars, trucks and motorcyclists: "Stay to the right, I told you! It's always you in the middle. To the right, to the right, understand? Do you want me to send you home?"

In Adrano, a sick child, blondish, very pale, pretty (a kitchen chair has been placed on the sidewalk especially for her; she sits smiling, flanked by two or three plump girlfriends who look after her as if she were a child of theirs): "No, leave me alone, the sun can't hurt me. Here they are now.... Yes, yes, look at them over there, in the distance...they're coming! What beautiful colors they are wearing! They look like flowers...."

A very ancient arthritic olive tree, bent out of shape, to a much younger companion: "Vanitus vanitatum, you say? You claim these Giro participants are fools because they're happy to hurt themselves for nothing, to race as if possessed by the devil, for no reason at all? And the others? Aren't they worse, the others, who say they must struggle for serious things? I prefer these guys, believe me, at least they have the courage not to promise their fellow men too complicated a paradise. They race for nothing, it's true, they are not putting anything together. However, how do you explain that the people, even the locals who are gloomy by nature, look so happy on seeing them?"

Ambrosini, the race director, who we spoke about earlier, is still tirelessly waving his little red flag: "You again? Is it possible you haven't yet understood you must stay to the right! To the right! To the right!"

A large handwritten placard, brandished above the crowd in Bronte: "Coppi, best wishes from your friends."

Mount Etna: "Still the same rotten luck! It's nineteen years since the Giro came through Sicily. This year, it has finally come. In fact, it's even been kind enough to circle around me, today it is actually going to climb on my back. Wouldn't you know I'd catch a cold. For two days I have been trying to chase away these stinking clouds that are covering my head and blocking my view. I can see nothing. Not even one of those brave boys have I been able to see. But I feel them passing over my body; they race over me: They are like a lot of swiftly moving ants. But did I see them? Not at all."

A child, perched on top of a little wall, addressing the occupants of a car: "Who's leading? Is Corrieri there? Who's leading?" (The motorists vanish after replying with a vague gesture.)

A lava gnome, emerging from an immense black, petrified cloud of smoke: "Something must have happened. Nasty business, I would say. A disaster, perhaps. Or it is Etna, that insane father of mine, who has started to vomit? If not, why are they racing like that?"

Miss Silvia Greenbed, sitting on the edge of a terrace in Taormina, addressing her mother: "Come, mommy, look at all those cars down there. Can you hear the noise? You'll see, mommy, they have captured Giuliano. Poor fellow! But why are they so set on tormenting him? He's so cute!"

Ambrosini, the implacable race director, his face redder than ever, waving his little red flag as hard as he can: "To the right! To the right! It's always the same ones!"

A policeman on a motorcycle in Messina's piazza Municipio, riding at walking pace, brushing against the enormous crowd overflowing from both sides of the finishing line, trying to keep them back: "Hey you, I'm talking to you, don't you dare lay a hand on me! Move back! Or do you want me to give you a couple of black eyes?"

A fan, thinking he sees at the end of the wide avenue a movement heralding an arrival, screams like a madman: "They're here! Here they are! Long live Corrieri! Cor-rie-ri! Cor-rie-ri!" (gradually diminishing, because it is a false alarm).

A young physician lost in the crowd with his wife, a niece and a child, a few minutes after the finish: "It's hard to believe. Yesterday, I stayed home and immediately heard on the radio who had won the stage, along with the complete order of arrival. Today I am here on the spot, I have been asking for ten minutes who came in first and have yet to get an answer!"

And guarding the port, the little statue of the Madonna, contemplating the spectacular, happy throng swarming in the sunshine: "My God! I have never seen so many people in my whole life. I didn't know, I really could not imagine I had so many human beings to love."

7

A SLIGHTLY CRAZY GRANDFATHER PEDALS IN THE WAKE OF THE CHAMPIONS

Cosenza, the night of May 23

I<small>N</small> M<small>ESSINA</small> <small>THIS MORNING THE RACERS BOARDED</small> the ferry and were extraordinarily excited by the strangeness of this sailing contraption, transporting in its stomach all these cars, with its little stairs, bridges, gangways, verandas, turrets, bars and small restaurants. They were like schoolchildren on an outing: they laughed, dumped glasses of water on each other from one terrace to another, forgetting what was waiting for them on the opposite shore. In the morning sun,  Calabria, with its delicate blue shadows, looked like one of those places pictured in the windows of travel agencies, radiating happiness. But behind this fairytale backdrop, the treacherous mountains were waiting. With its cargo of multicolored jerseys, the ferry sailed on. And meanwhile, in secret, someone had already crossed the strait, and astride his bicycle was laboriously, laboriously climbing toward Scylla.

In the piazza Municipio, the mayor of Villa San
Giovanni made a little speech befitting the occasion, candy
was handed out, then everybody set out walking. At that
hour and in that place, the world was wonderful. The sense
of being on a field trip was still prevalent, inspiring in the
giants of the road a touching emotion of self-indulgence.
Vertically, just below them, the sea was playing—yes, really—with the little rocks that outcropped near the shore; at
that very moment a young mermaid emerged from the water,
visible to her waist, she turned shamelessly toward the racers and laughed. Benso, the little imp on Bartali's team,
answered her with a gesture that was really suggestive. She
vanished, flipping her tail gracefully. And meanwhile, the
solo rider we mentioned earlier was pedaling ahead of them
as hard as he could, but he was visibly losing ground.

The sun dried the fishermen's nets that were spread on
the small beaches; smoke from a distant ship appeared on
the horizon, while a weird-looking stray dog with two tails,
one in the right place, the other hanging from its chest, trot-
ted for quite a while right in the middle of the procession; and
that showed how slowly they were pedaling. There were two,
three attempts to breakaway, involving Pasquini, Volpi,
Selvatico, Pasotti and others whose names escape us. But
the surrounding landscape was too beautiful. Even those racers lacking artistic sensibility were tacitly in agreement: to
start slaving away in such a place was tantamount to cursing.
It was like walking in a garden laid out above the bluest sea
ever seen: huge olive trees like cathedrals, daisies, flowers,
lawns, wheat and other plants, all green, and birds singing

more vivaciously than usual. The racers proceeded side by side on the wide ribbon of asphalt, as if they were only there to satisfy their curiosity, nothing more. And yet, despite their indolence, when they caught up with that solitary cyclist we mentioned, they passed him and left him miserably behind. One of the champions shouted something at him; what it was, we don't know because in these situations cars can stay in front of or behind the peloton, but not alongside it. But it must have been a witty phrase, since everybody exploded with laughter. And the other fellow was left more alone than before, and yet he kept on pedaling as hard as he could.

Which was not very hard. What can you expect from a fifty-seven-year-old man who, in the Giro's wake, yesterday and the day before, has covered the Palermo-Catania and the Catania-Messina routes over the mountains? Every year, they say, the Giro has its extra follower who, of his own free will, joins in the adventure and with Herculean efforts tries to compete with those who are really racing. Last year it was a soldier who had fled from his barracks; this time, it is an even more pathetic case, an old man, one can say, a certain Vito Ceo, a day-laborer living in Carbonara di Bari, who claims that in his youth he had broken the New York-Los Angeles bicycle record in twenty-five days. Setting out from Bari, with a racing bicycle, but without even a single spare tire and without a cent, he moved to Sicily during the past few days, and the day before yesterday he left early in the morning, well before the champions, to ride the same route as them. And he did reach Catania; his last ounce of strength used up, he had been obliged to spend the night at Regalbuto. But yesterday, from Regalbuto he pushed on as far as Messina. And this morning he got back in the saddle. Is he a madman, a maniac, a bicycle mystic, a sort of knight errant? And his wife—because Vito Ceo has a wife, two children, and a little granddaughter—what has she to say about it? "That woman, she's gross, she eats and drinks," he replies, taking from his pocket some mysterious, very greasy documents to prove he is a veteran cyclist. He wears a jersey bearing the name of the manufacturer of his bicycle, full knee-breeches, knee-length socks, a pair of sports shoes, and that's it. He is short, stocky, fat. A Don Quixote in the body of a Sancho Panza. He swears he will succeed in making it to Milan. And he pedals, pedals, slowly.

In the neighborhood of Mileto, the deafening noise of the caravan caused a little horse to flee madly across the fields. Natuzza Evolo, the young woman who "drips blood and hears voices," came out in front of her doorstep carrying one of her children (she had just finished ironing five scarves that, in her own blood, she had decorated with mysterious tiny outlines of saints, holy vessels, tree branches, and phrases in Latin).

"Who is leading? Are they far away?" we are asked by several seminarians wearing red sashes who were lined up along the shore. On reaching the sea, the road began to rear up, penetrating the greenish, inhospitable mountains. At last, as the climb cracked its whip, the lazy battalion stretched out, stretched to the point where it broke into numerous little pieces. And back there, who knows how far away by now, old Vito Ceo, the scatter-brained grandfather, the Don Quixote with Sancho Panza's face, was dragging himself, push after push on the pedals, along the wide deserted road.

The sun vanished. In its place, leaden skies. And no

more garden scenery, but dark ravines where nobody had any desire to linger. Now and again, a town appeared, incredible to find up there in such a remote spot, its houses in place and its crowd of people who asked us, the couriers, one thing: "Bartali or Coppi?" And in order not to disappoint them, as it was evident that any other option would have saddened them, we said not a word. Bartali and Coppi were not committing themselves. In the lead, well clear of everybody, two young unknowns, Pasotti and De Santi, were struggling up and down the fearfully steep inclines. The black rags hanging over a field to frighten away the swallows were a sign to Bartali, as if to encourage him; but Bartali did nothing more than was strictly necessary. De Santi, pedaling with all his might, caught up with Pasotti and took off alone. "Who is leading?" the people asked from all sides, their eyes gleaming. But we did not have the courage to reply. And, meantime, where was old Ceo? Had he collapsed on the side of the mountain, beckoning to the trucks to stop, or was he still holding on?

At the edge of the road two oxen, extraordinarily reminiscent of Carducci[9], stood motionless, staring at the bottom of the valley, that is, in the opposite direction, and they didn't turn their heads even one millimeter when the storm of cars passed right by where they were yoked. The road pushed on into a sort of thicket that, I would swear, judging by its aspect, was inhabited by hyenas and bandits, but nothing evil came out of it. Even though he had almost reached the end of his strength by now, De Santi gamboled alone toward Cosenza: through Soveria Manelli, Marzi, Rogliano. Then came a long straight

9. Carducci, a famous 19th century Italian poet, wrote a poem called "Il bove" ("The Oxen").

stretch, one last, fast climb. De Santi was first to cross the finish line, winning the stage but not the local savings bank's one hundred thousand lire awarded only for a two-minute advantage. So, only thirty-six seconds later, Pasotti arrived. Another minute-and-a-half, and the main group, which had been left behind, was there. Even before he had a chance to get his feet on the ground, Bartali fell under the avalanche of his admirers, taking a hard knock. The Italian-American Di Bacco was disqualified from the race because of having been towed by a car with the license RC4730. Vittorio Seghetti picked up a letter here from his fiancée, who tells him between the lines that they will never get married if he doesn't put some money aside, referring with due delicay to the chance of his winning at least a few cash prizes. And because of an illicit push in the sprint, Mario Fazi lost seven placings in the stage results.

And the grandfather? It is nine o'clock, and he has yet to show up. Will he get here before midnight? Are we to imagine him defeated and humiliated, a gasping wreck, picked up by a compassionate trucker, to be delivered to his home as if he were a piece of furniture? Or can we believe in the victory of a simple soul over the excessive wickedness of old age? I seem to see him in the heart of the black forest, struggling on, clumsy, ridiculous, but heroic. Take heart, old Ceo. You don't see them, but the spirits of the dead great champions have come toward you, and with ghostly legs pedal evanescent racing cycles. They too are old and decrepit, very tired, and a bit crazy. They escort you silently. Now, to give you courage, the frogs of Calabria will sing you their little military marches; and to guide you all along the way, the lightning bugs, usually so tightfisted, will light their tiny lamps just for you.

NEITHER COPPI NOR BARTALI
STOPPED IN EBOLI *

Salerno, the night of May 24

EAR COPPI, ESTEEMED MR. BARTALI (AND I address him this way because I am a little in awe of Bartali: he pedals with a frown on his face, and he is never seen walking around, not even in the lobby or the corridors of his hotel; yesterday morning, for example, during the ferry crossing from Messina to Villa San Giovanni, all the racers were, so to speak, out in the open, very visible to the passengers and approachable, all except Bartali, and I am still asking myself where the devel he could have hidden). Dear Coppi and esteemed Mr. Bartali, then, he who speaks to you is, in cycling terms, a complete blockhead; he knows nothing about shifting gears, chainrings and cogs; he has no clear idea about racing strategy, and during the past days he has

* This is an allusion to Italian writer Carlo Levi's novel, "Cristo si e fermato a Eboli" ("Christ has arrived in Eboli").

had to ask questions that were so naïve they almost created a scandal. That being stated honestly, I add that your reasons are inviolable, I understand your responsibility to your respective companies that employ you, and to your teams. I know you respect them scrupulously. It would be idiotic, I admit, to compromise the final classification of a race as long and arduous as the Giro by yielding to the temptation of a beau geste. I measure, or at least I hope I know how to measure, the frightful exertion of a stage like today's from Cosenza to Salerno, 292 kilometers, almost all of them in the mountains, with a discouraging, uninterrupted succession of very steep climbs and descents that didn't let up for a minute; and then there was the violent storm that brought wind, cold, fog and rain, to say nothing of the depressing effect of the landscape, no doubt beautiful when the sun is out, but today, pallid, wild and repulsive. To impose similar stages, I heard it said to one of your colleagues, is tantamount to warning the racers: economize your efforts, be very careful to give your all if you don't want to ruin your health. I don't know if it's true. Certainly, if someone had led us along today's route and told us that about a hundred men would be able to cover it on bicycles without ever dismounting, at a speed slightly less than 30 kilometers an hour, I probably would not have believed it. I admit, finally, that for all practical purposes the way you tackled the race was sensible; along with the group, you committed yourselves only during the last kilometers in pursuit of Leoni who broke away down that last descent before Eboli with Bevilacqua and Cargioli: Between the two rows of emotionally charged spectators, you caught the three-man group, right at the

Salerno stadium's gates and, in the final sprint, the one with the most class came out on top: Coppi first; second Leoni who, they say, would have taken a normal sprint, but he had worn himself out with the unsuccessful break; third, and rightly so, Bartali. Which, all things considered, shows you are completely right.

Now, however, being the incompetent person I am, allow me to ask you a question: Did you get a good look at the people who were waiting for you as you went through Calabria? Do you remember those thousands and thousands of faces anxiously turned in your direction, regardless of age or trade, peasants, shepherds, mothers, masons, little girls, monks, police, decrepit old ladies, mayors, clerks, street sweepers, teachers, and that limitless number of children? You crossed deserted valleys in which one could really have said that Christ, who stopped in Eboli, never set foot. Yet, on the boulders, at the edge of the thickets, standing on the steep banks along the road, men and women were waiting for you. Many of them had trudged many kilometers just so they could welcome you, descending from remote villages perched on top of ancient crags. You went through incredible towns hanging lopsided on the lofty flanks of the mountain, with a main street sloping at least thirty degrees in places, absolutely out of a fairytale: looking at them from a distance, from the other side of the valley, who would ever have imagined that anyone up there was interested in cycling? You could say they were strange islands of humanity banished far from our world, improbably cities, pure mirages.

Nonetheless, those roads were packed on both sides with happy people. Yes, absolutely happy; that's how those people were, people we never even guessed existed; they had such candor and goodness of heart that you wouldn't find their equal in any other place. Even you two, surely, because you are not stupid.

Even if all of your intent were focused on your effort, you must have sensed instinctively what the Giro d'Italia means in those stretches of country? They were laughing, did you see how they were laughing? Yours was no longer mere sport and you were not just champions. Without a shadow of rhetoric, you were the incarnation of the affluent, happy world that finally came to say hello—just for a few seconds, it's true, but it came—to those ancient, forgotten dwellings. Even though it was storming, you brought up there the light of a sort of America. It was Milan, it was Turin, the wonderful cities of the North that remembered their distant, poor little sisters.

And do you know what those people asked the two of us riding in a car a few kilometers ahead of the champions? Whether or not they wronged the others, who perhaps were struggling more than you, they asked only two things, with an almost desperate eagerness, as if for them it were a matter of life and death. And Coppi? And Bartali? What are they doing? Is Coppi leading? Is it true that Bartali has left everyone behind?

Meanwhile, you were wisely husbanding your strength in accordance with a faultless plan. If some greenhorn broke away, one who could in no way create worrisome complications, you let him be. You placed yourselves in the best position in the center of the group, without straining yourselves. Between the two of you (even if this were only part of the plan), the proverbial tension was no longer there. You, Bartali, you had at least three flat tires today and no one deigned to attack. Wise management, I repeat. But those people, those simple souls, resembled us a bit in that we are donkeys when it comes to bicycle racing. They believed in you blindly, they considered you heroes, idols, unbeatable beings. They found in you a reference point to the absurd dreams that each of us, no matter how humble, allows himself to have. They couldn't believe you were not in the lead, alone, shooting off in a dashing break. You are the most talented, aren't you? So why weren't you racing in the front?

It was senseless, I know. Why should we expect that one of you, and no one else, would be in the lead down there, at the bend, in each of those towns, and win all the stages, always leaving your companions behind on the climbs? There has never been and there never will be an athlete capable of doing that. I was not being reasonable. A little like the amateur who would like to see the great chess champions make ingenious moves in every game, while it is well-known that duels between great masters of chess are actually an epic poem of boredom, characterized by excessive preoccupation of avoiding every risk and impulse. You do your job on the basis of wise rules of which you have complete mastery. And today, too, it all turned out for the best. But be honest, my dear Coppi, my dear Bartali: Wouldn't it be better, since you can, to do a bit more? From a rational point of view it would probably be a ridiculous error. However, you would make many people happy! Wouldn't this also be a bargain, after all? And how much more they would love you! Think, once in a while, about those children, those little girls, those old people, those police officers, those peasants, those priests who yesterday and today waited for you; think of the inhabitants of Rosarno, Vito Valentia, Còraci, Rogliano, Tarsia, Lauria, Lagonegro, Auletta and Eboli: the way they looked at you, smiled at you, suffered agonies for you. Think about it sometime.

On the other hand, I may be wrong. The day after tomorrow, on the road to Naples, both of you are quite capable of contradicting me magnificently. In conclusion, carry on as if I said none of this.

9

ENTRY FORBIDDEN
TO THE CHAMPION'S ROOM

Amalfi, the night of May 25

T IS NOON AND THE CHAMPION IS STILL SLEEPING. Why is he so tired, the very one who needs exhaustion to feel well? All the others are out, riding around Salerno; luckily today the sun came out, and people are already seated at the café tables under canopies of vines, while the street players pay their respects by singing the most classic songs, free of charge. Yesterday's stage wore him out, perhaps. No, no, replies the little group of his courtiers in the hotel lobby. It's not that he's 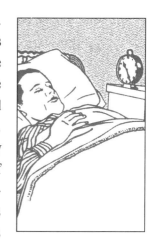 sleeping in the literal sense of the word. In fact, he is awake, they say, but he is still in bed, he doesn't feel like getting up, that's all. He'll have lunch in bed, too.

Then he is not feeling well? His wonderful body, which the doctors have studied uttering cries of amazement, is perhaps showing some slight dysfunction, however small? Is he feeling the after-effects of the fall at the Cosenza finish? Outside, the sun is shining. Fausto Coppi, in a chic, blue short-sleeved shirt and long trousers, is pedaling sluggishly at no more than seven kilometers an hour in the neighborhood of Amalfi, where he is staying; he's enjoying the fantastic spectacle of those houses set at dizzying heights, those Wagnerian crags, that sea worthy of Homer. Why is his great rival still in bed on such a day?

No, no, don't say that, not even in fun—his courtiers reply with amused smiles—as a matter of fact, he has never felt so well. He is in bed in a manner of speaking. In fact, he is not in bed at all. He got dressed quite a while ago, and the doctor who gave him his daily check-up did not find a hair out of place. There isn't the slightest hint of any weakness. It's just that he prefers to stay in his room, he doesn't want to see anyone. Is he in a bad mood, then? Discouraged? Bad news? A bit nervous? His guardians, custodians, lieutenants, advisors shake their heads. Nerves? But nerves don't exist for him. In his case, the cardio-muscular system carries him, confirming his net superiority decidedly over all the others. Uneasiness, anxiety, apprehension, fear are meaningless words for him.

So? On the ground floor of the hotel two teams of cheerful cyclists are seated at a table. Not him. A trusted waiter or, more prudently, even his personal masseur, enters the room furtively, bringing lunch on a tray. Through the front door the fans, thanks to the prodigious sensitivity that distinguishes them, glimpsed the sparkle of the soup tureen and the dishes being carried across the lobby. Bartali's lunch! And a shiver runs through the little crowd that has been waiting patiently since the early morning hours, giving them new hope. The great news is quickly spread.

How odd! All the other racers who just dismounted from their saddles and are seen at the restaurant, for example, or in the coffee shop, are difficult to recognize, so different do they look. Like actors who, having removed their make-up, are no longer acting and rejoin the ranks of ordinary men like us. Not him. Even after the race he does not go back to being just any man. He remains a "champion," alien to our everyday world. And the strange thing is that we thought this myth-phenomenon was destined exclusively for the naïve crowds. In the intimacy of his own circle, we believed, he will be considered a superior class cyclist, yes, but as a man, like all the others. Isn't it the same for great artists and powerful political figures? Seen close up in their daily life, they too come down from their pedestals. Respect becomes blurred, we're on first-name terms, we can take the liberty of joking. Instead, in Coppi's and Bartali's case, especially the latter, the myth persists even here among those close to them. Not that they are considered geniuses, but no one dares to have a poor opinion of them.

We consider everything they do in a special way, even the team directors on whom they depend, even the patriarchs of the bicycle, even the journalists, whose job almost always turns them into ruthless skeptics, have a not uncommon respect for the two champions without their realizing it. They deny it, of course, and if by chance they read these lines they will be inclined to laugh. Yet, it is true. And a doubt came to us: The spectators, even those in the front row, even the shrewdest and most irreverent, do they not perceive in the extraordinary abilities of the two men—unrefined abilities, if you will, rudimentary, essentially physical—the presence of something mysterious, sacred, a kind of grace, the sign of a supernatural authority? And this may explain the immense attraction of sport. This would justify what otherwise would seem absurd: to wit, that reasonable, well-educated people can lose their heads and get upset and scream over a football player or a cyclist. But there are those who will say: But isn't it frightening that the modern world gives vent to its secret charge of mysticism in the terraces of a stadium? Isn't it humiliating? It is difficult to answer, to be sure. It may be, however, that sports fanaticism, with all its extravagance, is a lot less vulgar than it seems at first glance.

The champion remained shut up in his room. He ate, let himself be massaged, read the mail, skimmed through the newspapers, talked for a long time with the few persons who entered the room, spoke complainingly of the bump he took the day before yesterday, protested about the racket down in the street the crowd was making as they continued to call for him, and grumbled about everything. And he abruptly went from one subject to another, without ever getting tired. If there is anyone who never gets discouraged during a race, Bartali is the one. Even if the day is a very bad day and he loses several minutes, he holds on. It almost seems as if— and perhaps his faith plays a part—he finds a sort of bitter comfort in suffering. And that he perceives in his misfortune a sign that Heaven is talking to him.

However, it is said that with the passing of time he is becoming strangely more intolerant of superfluous visits, of overly enthusiastic admirers, of the hundreds of irritations life inevitably inflicts on him. Who knows? Who can fathom the depths of his soul? Is glory itself beginning to frighten him, causing him to meditate on the future?

Meanwhile, the rest day has ended. The usual rites pertaining to the eve of a race begin again. In one of the hotel lounges, now deserted because everybody has gone to bed, Virginio Colombo, Bartali's team director, prepares race food for the members of his team. He has set out on a table seven slips of paper, on each one the name of a racer, and with the accuracy of a pharmacist, accordingly allots to each the prescribed foodstuffs.

"Do they all get the same portions?" I ask.

"Of course, identical portions for everyone."

"And why," I say, "for Bartali are there four portions of omelet roll-ups, while Benso has only three?"

"No, that's impossible."

"What do you mean, impossible? Count them."

Colombo counts them, and is a bit disconcerted. "So, you are right. I made a mistake." And he gives Benso an additional portion.

Was it an involuntary, almost instinctive, injustice? Sometimes it happens. But it is not only the portions of omelet. There are also more bananas for Bartali: four instead of three. And Colombo is worried, he realizes that we have noticed, he looks at us suspiciously.

"And the bananas?" we ask.

"What about the bananas?"

"Oh, nothing, nothing."

To persist would be spiteful.

FOR A MOMENT IT SEEMED
THAT BARTALI WAS BEATEN

Naples, the night of May 26

ARTALI WAS DROPPED. ON THE PRATOLA HILL, 50 kilometers out of Salerno, Fausto Coppi pedals with all his might. He is at the head of a group of a dozen racers, none of them members of his team; but he goes past alone. "And Bartali?" people ask. "Bartali is not there. Is Bartali in the second group?"

Sunshine, verdant hills, a monk, pine trees, vineyards, three more monks under a poplar. A tiny girl clapping her hands. Sudden puffs of dust where the road is being repaired. Children of every imaginable age. A cripple in a wheelchair. Clouds moving in from the east. And under the little white cycling cap, his angular face, burnt red by the sun and the exertion. He looks behind him. Is anyone coming to help him? No, nobody.... He has already gained four-hundred dred meters...now five hundred, six hundred.

We who are riding in front are met by the questioning hands characteristic of the southerner, stretched out waving, the fingers joined and pointing upward. It is a peremptory, and almost indignant appeal. They have been waiting there for an hour and can't wait any longer, they must know. Who is leading? Who is winning? What are we doing here—their demeanor seems to say—if not to bring them news? Who is leading? Coppi. "Bravo," the boys yell, jumping up and down and punching each other to express their joy. At that moment they could have hugged us, they would have been willing to do anything to please us. Other faces, however, clouded over so quickly it was almost laughable. "And Bartali?" Bartali is back there. "Bartali left behind?" They shout at us, begging us to say it isn't true. We do not deny it, that's just how it is. But there is no time to argue. We fly at a dizzying pace through the countryside, past ever more new faces lined up by the thousands to our right and left, an endless tunnel of humanity at the highest pitch of excitement. They have forgotten everything: who they are, the work waiting for them, their illnesses, luxuries, unpaid bills, headaches, love, everything except the memorable fact: Fausto Coppi is in the lead and Bartali, lagging behind, continues to lose ground.

San Giorgio. It is siesta time, when midday somnolence reigns over the fields, and the streets are deserted, and the cow herd falls asleep in the shade of the huge beech, and in the silence of the kitchen we can hear the flies buzzing, and outside, the cicadas…. But today everyone is on the street. Not even the dogs are napping, and they dart madly here and there trying to survive the infernal ballet of cars rushing by. Coppi and the other ten racers have gone by. The second hand turns, turns, and the pursuers still fail to appear. There they are at last. Bartali is in the lead; he throws us an irritated glance, his face looks a bit swollen by the exertion, but the muscles are not contracted in pain. He, too, is alone; no one comes forward to help him.

The surrounding countryside is stupendous, a perfect image of serenity and high summer. And yet it may be here that a drama is unfolding. Perhaps amid these joyous fields the Giro is taking a decisive turn, and a heart will be broken. Bartali, old lion, is this the day that sooner or later had to come, is this your supreme hour after which the last collapse of youth begins? Has the spell been shattered right here, on a miserable hill only 585 meters high? Is the faithful genie that until now has accompanied you, taking you toward glory, no longer answering your call? Have you become a man like all the others?

Suddenly, you know. The mysterious talent will have to leave you. In the middle of a race, all at once, you will feel strangely alone: like a king at the height of battle who, on turning to issue orders, no longer sees his army, dissolved by magic into nothingness. This terrible moment will come. But when? You don't know. And it could be this very day, during one of the Giro's easiest stages, because fate is cruel and amuses itself by creating, ironically, the unexpected. At this point, the time gap is almost a minute-and-a-half. That is not enough: tires frequently go flat.

That could well be today, the famous Bartali's fatal hour, and twenty years hence we journalists, now grown old and outdated, will give an account of it, as if it were a fairytale, to our younger colleagues who have come to see us in the editorial office late at night.

It really looked then as if a great event in our cycling history were about to occur; the twilight of an era and the decisive passing of the crown from one head to the other. An atmosphere of anxiety hangs over the never-ending procession speeding by, over the crowds in the towns, over the sports enthusiasts in the distant cities where the radio had already broadcast the news. But the faithful genie had not betrayed him. Invisible, it was still at the champion's side. Bartali punctures, Bartali changes the wheel in ten seconds; Bartali hurtles off in pursuit, angrier and more obstinate than ever. Does he get any help from the large inscriptions written in his honor on the asphalt? Is he comforted by the voices calling his name? Probably not, judging from his disdainful indifference. It is still him in front, and he doesn't tire. Now, the gap decreases; and Bartali, at the far end of the road, already catches sight of the many-colored cars of the other teams, with spare wheels sparkling on the racks: a sign that the lead peloton is not far away.

Welcome. An unbelievably delirious crowd, balconies packed to the bursting point and looking as though they are about to collapse under the excess weight. All this brings Campigli's paintings to mind. Come on, Bartali, six more kilometers and the lead group will be caught. Perhaps Coppi got tired of making all the effort by himself. Neither was it to his advantage to wear himself out to help Cottur, the *maglia rosa*, the race leader, who was in his group. The drama fades away, tension drops, everything goes back to the daily routine.

Nor do the greatest vedettes react when Biagioni, continuing his sprint after the King of the Mountains line at Monte Sarchio (won by Leoni), bounds ahead, alone. The giants are not alarmed, anyhow, Biagioni is among the last riders on general classification. Thus, the young Tuscan has the joy of passing all by himself between two unbroken walls of swaying, black humanity flooding the final forty downhill kilometers, toward Caserta's majestic boulevards that seem to have been specially built for triumphant arrivals.

Whether or not the towns' centers are inhabited, an indescribable mass of people has materialized along the roadsides. As we pass at full speed, and as Biagioni gradually advances, we hear the roar like a wave behind us as it breaks, crashing madly. But is it possible that there are so many human beings in the world? Have the professors and the census takers perhaps made a tremendous mistake? It's much more than forty-five million inhabitants indeed, if all of Italy were like this.

Sucked up by this vortex of a crowd that little by little swelled up to proportions conceived only in dreams, Biagioni hurtled into Naples. Is there any need to repeat what the congestion was like in the Arenaccia stadium? And the thunder that welcomed the entrance of that little bicycle, all alone? And Leoni's quite elegant dash four minutes later, stealing second place from Luciano Maggini and Coppi? And the cheers, the flowers, the gaiety, the hugs for the champions? And the golden cloud of dust that turned Naples into a mirage?

11

THE GHOSTS OF ANCIENT CASSINO WAKE UP FOR THE GIRO

Rome, the night of May 27

HY WAS ANCIENT, NOBLE CASSINO NOT WAITING today for the Giro's racers traveling from Naples to Rome? It would have been so nice. On the contrary: There were no lovely girls at the windows, even the windows were missing, even the walls were missing where the windows should have opened; there were no multicolored festoons of shiny paper strung between the little, dilapidated, pink houses; even the houses were missing, the streets, too; there was nothing but shapeless

rocks cooked and bleached white by the sun, and dust, wild grass, brambles, even a few shrubs indicating that now nature was in charge here, to wit rain, wind, sun, lizards, organisms of the vegetable and animal world, but man was no longer here, the patient creature who for many centuries had lived there, worked, loved, procreated in the intimacy of the dwellings he had built for himself stone upon stone, and now, instead, nothing, nothing existed any longer.

But was there really no one any longer in that gigantic white scar gleaming savagely in the sunshine on one side of the valley? But yes, there were some humans, reduced to unrecognizable fragments, bone slivers or ashes, or still whole but buried under the shapeless rocks. An old man, perhaps, or a woman, or a young man who had absolutely refused to leave when the latest model of heavy artillery guns began the most meticulous and total demolition ever seen in the world, so that not even a two-meter stump of wall remained, not even the slightest bit of shelter behind which a short soldier had the chance to slip, everything was leveled as it was at the beginning of the world; more so, in fact, because originally there was probably a growth of trees and bushes.

"The Giro?" they replied. "But we here, the people of ancient Cassino, we are not ready, we lack everything necessary to welcome the racers decently. Be patient, we no longer have streets they can ride on, nor eyes to see them, nor voices to cheer them with, and not even hands for applauding them."

"Come, wake up! Only for a moment. Bartali is here, Coppi is here. Don't you want to see them, if only out of curiosity? Half a minute is enough, come, make a little effort and then you will go back to sleep. They go fast, the giants of the road, you barely manage to get a glimpse of them and they are gone" (but this is a lie because today the giants of the road, our devourers of kilometers, our human locomotives, looked more like indolent slugs as they ambled along in amiable groups, chatting, not even thinking about doing battle; and only at the last moment, almost at the gates of Rome, will there be the obligatory attack by young men full of hope, but the aces will not put themselves out about it, so that the eight rebels—Ricci, Frosini, Pasotti, Rossello Vincenzo, Schaer, Busancano, Cerami, Dubuisson—will arrive at the Appio velodrome with a small lead and cross the finishing line in the order mentioned above).

"No, no, let us sleep," the voice replied, "go ask the others, those who stayed some distance away, see? There, where the valley widens.... They are starting to rebuild there. The new Cassino, I mean. It is already rising. They've worked hard, haven't they?"

"We see, yes, but it is something very different. A stirring, quite beautiful proof of human tenacity. However, this hideous, prison-like architecture has nothing to do with the city from the old days. It isn't even logical because life in such ugly houses will always be sad and uncomfortable. This is not Cassino. It is a strange, different creature that makes the scar on the side of the valley stand out even more cruelly."

"I understand," the voice said, "but it is too late. If we were to rise again, even for a minute, it would terrify the living. They remember us and love us, as long as we remain silent and quiescent underground. Too much time has gone by. The years erase everything. Just here is where my room used to be, my bed, my favorite saint's picture, the corn cob hanging on the wall, the rifle, two or three books, the stand with the basin, now there is a hazelnut tree, and robins hop around in its branches. It is better this way, perhaps. And better to abandon the Giro."

"The Giro? What's that?" asked Martin J. Collins, awakened by the ear-splitting racket of the Klaxons and the noise of the bicycles, and once a soldier attached to ammunition supply and now a bloodless ghost settled here for all time. (There had been a white flash, a great cloud of dust, a tremendous explosion, and nothing remained of the handsome young man, not even his helmet, himself dust, in fact, a vague memory.) And with difficulty he raised his sleepy head from his rustic tomb of rocks and wind and sun.

"Was ist los?" asked a voice a meter away from him, the voice of former feldwebel Friedrich Gestern, he, too, transformed into pure remembrance by a masterful shot. He was sleeping, he was awakened by the noise of the cars. He rubs his tired eyes so he can see better. And others, invisible to us, wake up along slopes that have become green again, in the small valleys that today, in the May sunshine, can look like tiny paradises and five years ago were crawling with corpses. How many there are! A massive army of mixed uniforms and races, men who butchered each other and who now live side by side in peace, reconciled by the supreme armistice.

"Not to worry," we say to them, "it's the Giro, brave men; it harms no one. These boys pedal, exert themselves, try to race (except for today) as fast as they can. And why? For nothing. For the pleasure of finishing first, for the satisfaction of those who are there to watch them because if man isn't fighting in one way or another he becomes unhappy. But pardon us, perhaps this is not something for you…. It is life, that's what it is, in its most ingenuous, sensational form, and for you somewhat irritating, I'm afraid. Pardon us.

"We were passing by. If we have awakened you, we are

sorry. We wanted only to say hello to the old Cassino that no longer exists. And you know a thing or two about that. Do not be afraid, we are leaving right away, then you won't see us again for at least another year. Sleep well, my children!"

And the caravan of the champions (not champions today, though), with its sacriligeous voices, filed by below the horrendous scar, and vanished into the green countryside; very soon not even its echo could be heard. Back there in Cassino, at the far end of the valley, the masons started hammering again, time began to pass once more over the shattered rocks of the whitish rubble following the side of the mountain.

The haggard specters lay down again, rested their cheeks against the compassionate earth, and went back to sleep. And us, we looked at the swarm of racers, so cheerful with all those colorful jerseys and sparkling bicycles, we looked at the people quivering with impatience, the traffic policemen bustling to regulate the retinue's speed, that whole little world galloping madly toward the north of Italy. The sunshine was splendid, it was hot. And then, they will ask us, "Are they all still in a group?"

12

A BREAK THAT TAKES YOUR BREATH AWAY, FROM ROME TO THE ADRIATIC

Pesaro, the night of May 28

T IS A BITTER THING TO CROSS THIS PART OF ITALY, from Rome to Pesaro, without time to take a breath, and not being able to stop. This is Italy at its most Italian, where a hundred thousand memories of great events are remembered, even by those who went only to the elementary school. But also by those who have never been to school and do not carry within themselves any trace of all that has happened over the centuries, this extraordinarily humanized land speaks to

the illiterate as well. And unless one is a savage, one would want to stop and at least relax in the shade of a tree, to listen to the music of the little birds and gaze at the clouds happily sailing above the castles, whose battlements are open to the flight of swallows.

Nothing in the world is more antithetic to speed than

this solemn landscape whose respiratory rhythm is measured in centuries. They weren't in a hurry today, either, these cities and towns, so ancient as to seem as much a part of the landscape as a forest or cliff.

But we did stop. Many predicted that the Giro's longest stage, two hundred ninety-eight kilometers, would be limited to a lethargic outing ending—we should recognize—in a brief skirmish during the final kilometers. The one hundred seventy-six legs leaving at seven o'clock from the Ponte Milvio would grind along the never-ending road, it was felt, with the speed of a barbarous old organ grinder. On the contrary, there was no respite. From beginning to end: a frenetic flight that kept the reporters' ears perked up without a moment's rest, launched cars and motorcycle messengers in the wild breakaways, and it was sealed by an exceptional average speed. Old Belloni, team manager for Ronconi and companions, said he could not recall—and in his day he certainly took part in some hellish gallops—such frantic pace during that long a stage. The average was in fact more than thirty-seven kilometers an hour. If a similar thing happened during the Tour de France—someone said this evening— who knows what a great fuss they would make about it.... Therefore, we didn't have a minute to contemplate the view, to listen to the learned quotations of our colleague who's a genius in history, to greet with customary consideration the new towns and regions running toward us. And at the source of the Clitumnus there was not a single person who responded to the inviting gestures of the six or seven nymphs, charming, in truth, who showed themselves at the edge of a thicket, smiling.

The powder that set off the explosion that, from Rome to the Adriatic, continued like the flame of a fuse, was the Terni intermediate sprint. The intermediate sprints are an innovation for the Giro, adopted despite it being considered controversial. These are finish lines set up in the middle of the stage that award to the winner a one-minute bonus (half-a-minute to the second, fifteen seconds to the third), exactly the same as for a stage finish. The new idea worked. And the patron of the Giro, Emilio De Martino, is extremely satisfied with it. It was a success that, from the beginning, launched a series of escapes: by Vicini and Bevilacqua, briefly; then by Ronconi and Pasquini; then by Monari and Ricci. From the main pack, small groups of two or three racers detached themselves, each time attempting to breakaway. Several were able to maintain the pace and managed to catch up with the others already in the front, or else, they dangled halfway across until they were again swallowed up by the main group. A tense atmosphere, then, starting from Rome's suburbs, and even more tense when, with the lead patrol having been reinforced by the presence of twenty racers, the giants who remained behind found themselves at one point eight minutes back; and it looked as though a hard blow was in store for the two great ones.

At Terni, under the banner of the intermediate sprint line, the first to pass, his red head bent in the agony of his final effort, was Vicini, followed by Pasquini and Ronconi. There were three of them, alone, but following were about twenty more, determined to catch up with them. Coppi and Bartali hesitating, the riders taking part in this break that was limited in scope from the start—that is, the intermediate stage—took on new life and attempted what no one had probably expected: maintain the gap for two hundred kilometers more, as far as the velodrome at Pesaro. The result was the very fast pace that amazed even Cleto Radice, the prince of timekeepers.

And all along the route, the people who rushed to welcome the Giro were magnificent. You couldn't compare them, however, with the astonishing crowds in Sicily and Calabria, so anxious, happy, and at the same time respectful, that they seem to have been painted on either side of the road, so perfectly were they aligned. Today, in comparison, it looked as though people had a poor opinion of the giants of the road, a relatively poor opinion, to be sure, since the boys were not stingy with their praise traced in chalk on the asphalt, or in crayon on the walls, or in ink on small placards lifted on long broom handles and almost thrust in the faces of the racers to make sure they could read them. For example: "Long live Bartali, the conqueror" or "Bartali, make them all cry on the Izoard!"

Did the multicolored mob of road cyclists know they were riding through one of the most beautiful regions in the world? Would it have made any difference if they had been surrounded by the foggy suburbs of an industrial basin? Surely it was a crime, in a certain sense, to make use of such enchanting scenery for such unrewarding, bestial hard labor. Unaware, without looking around them, the runaways had eyes only for the pails of water that thoughtful spectators set out in front of their houses to refresh them a little, as they gobbled up the kilometers. We in the car saw something—hasty, interrupted images of this fundamental Italy of great, malleable beauty—the Italy, that is, of majestic ruins heavy with history, the Italy of oak and cypress trees, of immense patrician villas perched on slopes like so many weary empresses, the Italy of embossed walls covered with coats of arms, of the shaky, worn-out country buses hurtling vertiginously down into the valley depths, the Italy of ancient churches, of rail crossing keepers' tiny lodges, of young pregnant women, of the stonecutters working at the roadside under the midday sun, of Madonna statues set into the corners of houses, their little votive lamps always lit, the Italy of haystacks and majestic, long-horned oxen, of bearded young monks passing by on bicycles, of cliffs too picturesque to believe nature alone produced them, of bridges thousands of years old and still capable of carrying on their backs huge haulage trucks, the Italy of hostelries and accordions, of grandiose palaces of the nobility converted to barns and stables, of gentle hills covered with cypress trees to their summits.

We saw a few fragments of it, almost by fraud. They, the cyclists, nothing. The cyclists were pedaling, furiously chewing calorie-laden food because it's necessary straightaway to replace the energy discharged, to turn the wheel hubs. The three fugitives became seven; a little past Foligno, the seven became almost twenty. Then, the twenty thinned to just fifteen because not all of them were capable of supporting the effort. The duel was reduced to its simplest terms: in the lead, a group including Leoni, Ronconi, Fazio and Pasotti, who promised a lot and threatened a violent upheaval in the overall classification; a little behind, the main body of the expedition.

And the aces? The aces know what they are doing. The aces are astute, and even more astute and insightful are their team managers. The aces, the two great ones, we mean to say, are very wealthy where strength is concerned, and like all self-made wealthy people they are also a bit miserly. Why spend more than is necessary? When the right moment comes, in the Dolomites, for example, or the Alps, up there, where cunning and trickery are of no value, then they will empty their bags, and they will pay down to their last cent. This, say the well-informed, is more or less their strategy.

For the time being, they limit themselves to the indispensable: to reduce as they did today, for example, within the limits of safety (less than two minutes) the gap between them and the first of the runaways, to keep an eye on one another, to not allow any risky, surprising turn of events. But what does it matter then if the pink jersey is switched from one cyclist to another and if this evening Cottur (who at night stashed the jersey under his mattress to ward off bad luck) had to pass it on to Fazio? What does it matter if at every stage this or that name appears in the newspaper headlines? Let the most brilliant, handsome Leoni have a good time breaking away as he did today and showing off as he did today one of his irresistible sprints, winning the stage. The right moment—they seem to be saying—will come. And meanwhile, they are conserving their strength....

Editor's note: Buzzati did not report on the next stage, Pesaro-Venice, because the Corriere della Sera *was not published on Mondays. To fill in the gap, we have inserted the report submitted to the* Corriere d'Informazione *by Ciro Verratti, its sports correspondent.*

DOUBLE VICTORY FOR CASOLA , AT VENICE AND THE INTERMEDIATE SPRINT

Venice, the morning of May 30
[This stage reported by Ciro Verratti]

THERE IS A DIVINE COMMANDMENT THAT SAYS "Remember to keep the Sabbath day holy," and the Giro's racers, thinking that yesterday was Sunday, must have remembered it. In fact, this was a stage during which no one worked, since a bicycle promenade on a Sunday is not work; even ordinary mortals do it, boys and girls, office workers and students, professional people and retirees. It's true that it was a rather long promenade, and now and then there were some small sprints that caused some splits, but as far as length is concerned, two hundred seventy-three kilometers for these men is a trifle, particularly when there are no climbs and the accelerations caused by the sprints were not obligatory and the cyclists involved were only those who had the fame and responsibility of being a team's best sprinter.

In point of fact, it was to Casola's great benefit because he had a pinch of dynamite in his calves, and every time he attacked he succeeded in putting his own wheel ahead of those of his rivals. And so he won two stages: the intermediate sprint at Ferrara and the real finish in Venice. As a result of these two successful sprints, he picked up two minutes in the general classification, two minutes that are normally only earned by sweating blood and slogging tens and tens of kilometers alone. The truth is that Casola has developed a first-class technique, like a track sprinter, and apart from the lightning speed of his jump, a gift of nature, he has the intelligence to choose his position and, more important, to know the exact moment to make his move.

With this good-hearted, easy-going boy, a true little devil in the peloton, you're sure to have fun. When some innocent prank is being planned, when some buffoonery is being put together, you can be sure he is the director; but if there is a finishing line of some worth, if there is a sprint requiring commitment, you can be equally sure that Casola never shies away. During yesterday's promenade, he was the most entertaining and the most compelling beneath the finishing-line banners, those, naturally, that were worth the effort. It's just a pity that those two minutes are of no use to him; considering his placing he could very well donate them to someone else.

Of course, the route was not one of those that seemed to have been invented deliberately by nature to favor planning breakaways or encouraging audacious attacks. After the first breakaway attempt following the stage start, that is, after the little Siligate hill separating Pesaro from Cattolica that climbs just high enough to give one a panoramic view of the countryside, all the rest was nothing but smooth asphalt, without a rise, perfectly level. The Sunday crowds, which make the Giro a more enjoyable, festive event, were cheering the racers all along the route, calling out the names of the aces, but the aces, as you know, pay no attention to this nonsense; they pretend not to even notice the banners singing their praises, on which the creative imagination of the *tifosi* gives you a warm heart.

We read on one placard attached to a pole a highly metaphoric message: "Coppi, with your legs of steel and your aerodynamic nose, you are our consolation," and farther ahead we saw one similarly dedicated to the crowd's other favorite: "Bartali, when you are on the Izoard, make them all cry." The aces are not moved, so hardened to celebrity have they become, and those placards, prepared so carefully and imaginatively in the cafés frequented by sports fans, are read only by some bored members of the caravan who have time to look around because of the slow-moving pace of the race.

Yesterday, in fact, no inclination to do battle, no desire for glory stimulated the racers, and the rhythm of the race, particularly at the beginning, was so sluggishly bourgeois that three or four youths who slipped undetected among the caravan's cars and were pedaling furiously, so overjoyed were they to find themselves part of the Giro that they suddenly had to apply their brakes in order to avoid running into the real racers. They most likely boasted to their friends about the exploit, but perhaps in their heart of hearts they were probably a little disappointed with the giants of the road. Despite all this, the average speed was fairly high, and judging by the welcome extended to the race in Romagna and the Veneto, one must conclude that the Giro d'Italia, whether it passes at a frenzied pace or with the lassitude of a tourist, it always arouses incomparable enthusiasm, and thrills fans and observers alike.

Unfortunately, yesterday's race claimed a victim: Mario Vicini. Near Rimini, this vigorous young racer enjoyed a happy family reunion. His wife and three children, a charming young lady and two lively boys, came to meet him; and since the pace was rather slow he got off his bicycle so he could give them a hug. A small crowd had gathered around them to admire this idyllic picture, and also there to welcome him were Mario's friends and neighbors, who were thrilled to be in his company. Then he got back on his bicycle, smiling and serene, and pumping with his long, piston-like legs, he had no trouble catching up to his companions.

Everybody was pedaling in a relaxed, nonchalant manner; and the Rimini sprint, where Casola took the first success of the day, did no more than cause a faint ripple. We had arrived at Ravenna's gates when we saw Vicini suddenly fly off his bicycle and fall heavily to the ground, where he remained motionless, blood pouring from his head. All the cars in the caravan veered sharply to avoid him, then several people stopped to help the injured racer. But Vicini was unconscious, a wound to his temple bleeding profusely. He fell off because a tubular tire had suddenly come off the rim, and his head had struck a rock on the roadside. A police car took him immediately to the hospital in Ravenna, where he was diagnosed with multiple head injuries, a cranial trauma and a fractured left collarbone. At present there is no sign of brain damage, but it was certainly a very hard blow; so he was eliminated from the race on roads that were familiar to him, and where the warmest applause awaited him.

We got back on the road and went on to Ferrara at a reduced speed. This time not even the intermediate sprint managed to shake off the Sunday sluggishness. At Argenta there had been a breakaway attempt by Schaer, Pasquini, Ausenda, Cargioli, Vittorio Magni and Pasquetti, but the group had reacted vigorously, bringing those madcaps quickly back in line. At the Ferrara sprint line, we have already described how Casola managed to win the one-minute bonus; he was followed by Conte, Leoni, Bevilacqua and Luciano Maggini, in that order. Then the racers immediately regrouped, and nothing disturbed the march until Padua, where there was a third traffic jam and we saw the big team cars among the racers. Vittorio Rossello and De Santi took advantage of the situation to dash happily away for a few kilometers, but once again the group hit the pedals hard and went after the two reckless boys.

The last episode was the finish in Venice, on the Lagoon bridge. A magnificent finale on a highway forty meters (one hundred thirty feet) wide that would have accommodated a safe sprint even by an entire regiment. Casola took off from some way out, accelerating progressively, and Leoni, who in truth, had some trouble extricating himself from the group, tried in vain to come back to him on the right. He didn't make it, and Luigi Casola was first across the line, half a bike's length clear, lifting one arm toward the sky so the judges could clearly see he was the winner.

How does a Giro d'Italia arrive in Venice? We saw that yesterday. All the caravan's vehicles—the journalists' cars, radio stations' cars, the team cars, the publicity cars, the racers' gleaming machines—are loaded on large rafts and taken to the Lido. They had never seen anything like that on the Canale della Giudecca and in the San Marco dock, and they had never welcomed such a picturesque, priceless naval procession. The ferries' fog-horn sirens wailed their greetings to us, the gondolas cheerfully came to meet us and applaud us, and the gondoliers, who are no connoisseurs of terra firma, saw Coppi and Bartali for the first time in their lives. Small miracles of the Giro.

14

THE VICTIMS OF THE "MAXIMUM TIME" RULE

Venice, the night of May 30

HEN THE FRONT GROUP, HEADS BENT, HAD MADE their last furious assault on the finishing line and the almost unbearable roar of the crowd had been reduced to numerous single cries, were less and less hysterical, and like a flood the first rows of spectators breaking through the protective cord had engulfed the still-gasping champions to embrace them, kiss them, touch them....

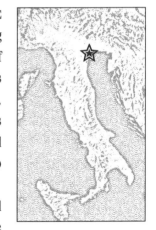

When the official timekeeper had pressed the button on his stopwatch, and the finish-line judges—we will never understand how—had determined the order in which the racers had finished in the middle of the sprint's crazy confusion, and the glass negative recording the finish sprint had been sent to be developed and used to clarify the almost certain disputes....

When the photographers had taken pictures of the winner holding the bouquet of flowers, fraternally embraced by mysterious gentlemen who were probably seeing him for the first time, but who tried in this way to gain a scintilla of reflected glory and whose friends would turn green with envy the next day as they were shown pictures in the newspapers, their faces stunned and triumphant, the winner at their side....

When the journalists, in strange, brightly colored coveralls and little red baseball caps they wouldn't dare wear on the streets of their city for fear of being teased, had reported in front of a microphone, on the radio, or from the closest public telephone the last phases of the stage and the order of finish, their voices as excited as if they were announcing the explosion of the first atomic bomb....

When the top aces, having freed themselves energetically from the thousands of too enthusiastic hands trying to grab them (in all that uproar there were even some who—insane!—held out to them a postcard and a pencil, begging them for an autograph), had been lifted with great effort into their respective team cars to be taken to the hotel (the colorful open-top cars bearing their sponsor's name down each side, and on the back of the strange-looking rack loaded with bicycles and spare wheels that, during the race, blown by the breeze, spin, spin like graceful little windmills); and after the throng, stampeding as if rushing to get to a safety exit during a bad fire, had poured into the adjacent streets to see them go by....

When the linotypists in distant cities had set the news into leaden lines, and the lines were put in a page, and from the page the matrix was drawn, and from the matrix the roller was fixed to the rotary press, and the presses were set in motion, and the first copies had appeared, with their bold headlines and the winner's picture, and the newsboys' strident shouts had been heard in the main streets by the men shut up in offices who, shaken by the tone of those shouts, wondered if by chance war had broken out....

When in the hotels—whose lobbies were alive with an indescribable confusion of porters, bicycles, journalists, team managers, telegraph boys, suitcases, inquisitive fans, American and Swiss tourists at the height of astonishment and embarrassment—the showers had started to work, pouring jets of water over the backs and necks of the champions, running down their limbs, dislodging the incrustations of dust and finally running murkily and grittily toward the drains; after the masseurs had started to put some tone back into the precious muscles of their charges lying on the beds, while from the street rose the exasperating chorus of the fans begging for a glimpse, however brief, of their idol....

When the press office at race headquarters had distributed cyclostyled copies of the stage results and the new general classification, and in a separate little room the international jury—four dignified big-wigs, two Italians, one Belgian and a Frenchman—had come to an overall agreement on the steps to be taken, such as: a 2000-lire fine to racer X (second violation) for an unauthorized feed from his team car and 5000 lire to the team itself for the same reason; a 500-lire fine to the racers listed below for an unsolicited push (second violation) et cetera, et cetera; a 500-lire fine to racer Z who, while having declared he was abandoning, had not removed his number as required; and so on....

When nobody in the caravan was left in the stadium and

the champions had started off toward their lodgings, either by car or alone in the saddle of their bicycles, and the spirited tension had dissipated entirely, and the immense crowd, so recently full of enthusiasm and energy, had become a weary flock (the happy young faces changed to limp masks, their eyes expressionless, their aching feet dragging) and streamed away amid the bestial racket of cars stuck in the traffic jam....

When the windows, from which a few minutes before had leaned marvelous, smiling young girls, had been closed and the inevitably sad post-holiday emptiness had invaded everybody's spirits—while the city was now, little by little, getting back to its normal activities, streetcars started to go by again, the policemen mobilized for the occasion returned to their barracks, and in the empty arena, once the scene of the triumph, the wind was scattering rubbish, old newspapers, crushed flowers....

When all this had taken place, three young men arrived on bicycles, dirty, perspiring, faces disfigured by exertion, trying to get through the rowdy, slow-moving river of people. "Excuse me, please, excuse me, please!" they shout. "Make way! Make way!" With desperate efforts they try to make their way without losing their balance. But the crowd is too dense. They have to put one foot on the ground, dismount, and push forcefully toward the entrance to the stadium. At first they are taken for three pitiful cyclists who, when races are being run, dress themselves like the real champions, putting on jerseys identical to theirs and, electrified by their example, swarm into the stadium at a mad speed, pinning their hopes on a misunderstanding; and in fact some do make the mistake, a few girls shout, "Well done," some myopic fans take them for Ronconi or Bevilacqua, it also happens that, from a distance, they are mistaken for a Coppi or a Bartali. But these three are not rushing away from the finish point; on the contrary, that's where they are going. And it is obvious they have covered a lot of ground, too much for them. They have a number pinned to their backs; and another number hangs from the crossbar of their bicycle.

Finally the crowd understands, moves aside to let them pass, and watches them. However, no one applauds, no one shouts their names, no one carries them in triumph. They are the latecomers, those who remained behind by dozens of kilometers the entire second half of the stage, so that instead of walls of enthusiastic humanity lining the roadsides, they met disorderly streams of people on their way back home. They are the last, the disinherited, the destitute, the afflicted, the pariahs, the unknown ones always at the dangerous edge of the maximum time limit (twenty minutes for every hundred kilometers). Waiting for them at the stadium's entrance there is perhaps a minor timekeeper, impatient to go and freshen up, who will record their arrival. But maybe there is no longer anyone there and they will have to beg the jury to be lenient, claiming plausible excuses such as a fall, the support vehicle's breakdown, an accident, anything whatsoever that might be qualified as *force majeure*. And perhaps the powers that be will turn a blind eye.

In truth, two of the distraught trio did not seem to take it too much to heart. Arriving late is just their job. They are the lowest-ranked *gregari*, required by their contract to give up their spare wheel to the team leader, to run back and forth from one farmstead to the other to fetch drinking water for him, to tow him if he is in difficulty, to wait for him if he is behind, to pick up at the feed zone, and take to him the cloth musette bag, containing provisions; a bit like hunting dogs running up and down that end up covering more ground than their masters.

When they have accomplished these humble tasks, it matters little whether they arrive among the first. On the contrary, the team manager prefers that they not go overboard: let them spare themselves, save energy for the next day, swallow their aspirations, arrive an hour late, as long as they don't exceed the maximum time allowed. They arrived last because of other people, in sum, precisely as they had been instructed to do.

But not the third one. Today he had not had to give everything to follow his team leader, taking him a bottle of water or orangeade, he did not hand over any wheels, he really sacrificed absolutely nothing to him. The third one did not stifle his ambitions. He really is defeated. He had a terrible bout of weakness, wasn't able to stay in the group's shelter, and the pep pill swallowed at the start of the last climb did nothing to help. His strength returned for about ten minutes, but afterward things got worse and worse. Collapsed, destroyed, a wreck. And while the other two still have the energy to curse the people blocking their passage, he follows silently, looking about him with a dazed expression. What happened to him? All around him impassive, unkind, alien faces from another world. His fiancée was waiting for him in the stadium, she had written him that she would be there. She, too, has probably left by now, or perhaps she is there, in the crowd, a meter away from him and she sees him but does not recognize him. Or else she has seen him and is hiding because she is ashamed of him: a proud girl like her engaged to the lowest of the lowly?

The sun is already setting amid dusty reddish halos, and the crowd continues to disperse. Increasingly congested streams of people pour against him as he struggles painfully. The other two cyclists, cursing, have managed to get through. Now he is alone. The people bump into him, tossed from side to side; a car, its siren wailing, obliges him to give way. Daylight fades, the street lights come on. "Where is the stadium?" he asks. They respond with vague gestures, almost annoyed. "Excuse me, excuse me," he begs, his voice almost inaudible. But it is already nighttime. How many hours have gone by since the first ones arrived? How many days? Or months? The night is dark, and beyond the crowd, the lights of the cafés shine out. And yet another throng, like a black stream of nasty, hostile lava flows toward him. "Where is the stadium?" he asks. "Which stadium?" they answer. "The one for the Giro d'Italia." "Ah, the Giro d'Italia...those were the days...." and they shake their heads pityingly. Not hours, not days or months: It's entire years that have gone by since the race finished. And he is alone. And it is cold. And his fiancée is out for a walk with someone else; or she may already be married.... "Where is the stadium?" he begs. "Stadium?" they reply. "Giro d'Italia? What does that mean?"

15

TRIESTE WEEPS AND REJOICES, COVERING THE CHAMPIONS WITH FLOWERS

Udine, the night of May 31

A T THE GATES OF TRIESTE, THE FINISHING LINE of the intermediate sprint was on the stupendous seaside promenade. Leoni, with one of his bird-like darts—you can see him suddenly breaking away from the lead group, his arms curved around the handlebars, looking just like a kite plummeting down on its prey—took the sprint ahead of Casola and Conte. Then, brought to life by the sprint, the group entered the city. At that point, the atmosphere of the Giro suddenly changed.

All at once, there no longer was any difference between one racer and the other, Bartali was on the same level as Carollo, Coppi equal to Malabrocca, Leoni to Brasola. Appearing from nowhere, we were suddenly met by fantastic views of crowds, swarming on roof terraces, a jubilant population, flowers raining from the sky, and flags,

flags, again and again. There was no longer any difference between the great champions and the vulgar nags, and not even between the racers and members of the caravan; the same went for Ronconi and the motorcycle messenger, Cottur and us, the reporters; we were truly equal. Because we all came from Italy. All that had happened before that moment lost its unimportance: the fact that Bartali and Coppi had not yet given battle, that since Venice the race had proceeded slowly, with a few brief thrills at the various sprints, where the successive winners were Bevilacqua, Casola, Pasquetti, De Santi, Cottur; and that thanks to the one-minute bonus for those intermediate sprints the pink jersey had virtually passed from the shoulders of Fazio to those of Leoni; for several minutes the overall classification had no importance, neither did the strategies of the different teams, nor the aspirations of the giants, nor the dreams of the young novices. One single thought dominated; even the champions understood and they pedaled as if they were on parade, forgetting they were rivals.

Three years ago, the Giro had come to Trieste the very day before it became a Free Territory. Furthermore, at Pieris there had been the well-known assault on the racers that brought the poignancy of that day to its highest point. There were extraordinary demonstrations in the city, a sort of farewell to the Fatherland, and those who were present narrate how even the most unfeeling people wept like children. Today, three years later, it was almost like a reunion for the people of Trieste, moments of tremendous joy and, at the same time, of bitterness because we went by like a whirlwind: no sooner were we glimpsed, than we had vanished.

Like someone welcomes his brother unexpectedly returning from a long exile, who is about to kiss him, and sees that he barely has the time to enter the house before he is already lifting his hand to wave goodbye because he must leave again immediately.

Today, at about two o'clock, Trieste was stirringly splendid, with its delicate cobalt blue sea, a white-hot sun and waving flags as far as the eye can see: the red, white and green fluttering everywhere. It's been quite some years since we had seen such a sight.

They shouted: "Hurrah for Coppi!" but it was something else they wanted to say, "Hurrah for Bartali!" and it was something else they were referring to, and not to Bartali. "Hurrah for the Giro's little guys, hurrah for Cottur, hurrah for Leoni!" they shouted, and it was always something else the people of Trieste referred to today, something that had more grandeur, that's felt more painfully, and that by now they had become accustomed to keeping well-hidden within themselves; today, they could at last roar it openly. And the racers, with numbers on their backs, understood they had all become equal, that they were only Italians and no longer champions, locomotives, human torpedoes; as one, they push forward amid all those powerful waves of love, forgetting they were enemies.

By chance, just the evening before, I was discussing with a colleague the concepts of patriotism, nation, European unity, et cetera. And he told me that the concept of Fatherland is now out-of-date; he assured us he felt that he was much more than simply Italian, he felt that he was a citizen of Europe—these are his very words—in fact, of the world, like Gary Davis. So I asked him if, for example, he would be sorry to see Italy wronged. He shook his head and asserted that in all fairness he was distressed whenever an injustice was done to any nation whatsoever, Italy or Sweden, or England, or even Persia. He maintained that he had freed himself from the old style patriotism as if it were a petty encumbrance, and in exchange he had acquired a new patriotism, much nobler, that embraced all of humanity. A highly gifted man, then, one must admit. But today, as we were passing through jubilant Trieste, I became engrossed in observing him closely. His car was right behind ours, so I was able to keep an eye on him. Oh, the citizen of the world, the philosopher soaring high above humanity's old, so naïve fundamentals. His lips were pursed up oddly in a way I had never seen before. He put on large black glasses, which he usually did not wear. The citizen of the world, full of shame, did not want to be seen. He was weeping. I swear that he was weeping.

The exclusive, ardent love for one's Fatherland that existed in the past is certainly out-of-date. But today in Trieste I have seen thousands and thousands of my fellow men waving, like flags, pieces of cloth, of every size, but all the same color; and waving them with all their might, so that we would be sure to notice them, until they were soon exhausted; they, too, like the racers, have their physical limit. Still, their faces calm, gritting their teeth, they held out; perish the thought that those little flags would stop waving until the whole caravan had disappeared completely: to them it would have been like a betrayal.

I saw grown men wiping their eyes with the backs of

their hands, seeing nothing through the veil of tears but mud-
dled blotches flying away in the dazzling sun. I saw young
men on motorcycles passing again and again, firmly holding
gigantic tricolors aloft in the wind; and who knows what an
effort it was for them! I saw the *cerini*—that is, the civilian
policemen in English-style dark blue uniforms, and the
British red berets—I saw them look around, astonished,
unable to believe their eyes. I saw an old lady on a balcony
greeting us as if we were her children; and she had put on her
record player that ancient song—do you remember it?—that
says "Oh, Italy, Italy, dear to my heart," and the strident voice
spilled out over the street, mysteriously overcoming the rumble of the cars and cruelly wrenching everyone's heart.

Then we climbed the hill leading to the Villa Opicina
across the first humps of the Carso, the still green and
romantic limestone massif, where we dipped down toward
Gorizia; here, the enchantment ceased, and we resumed our
daily routine. Doni—who is an adoptive citizen of Udine—
broke away with Biagioni and Frosini, and joined forces with
Leoni, Pasotti, Tonini, Pezzi and Castellucci. This group of
eight riders flew away, while the two super-champions, faithful to an order becoming stranger day by day, did not react.
So the eight men arrived in Udine about three minutes ahead
of their closest pursuers, Ronconi, Schaer and Fazio, and
more than four minutes ahead of the next group that included the aces.

But now, looking back, we can no longer envision—
and it is only a matter of two hours ago—the wild gallop
along the marvelous road from Gorizia, nor the impressive
array of people in Udine, nor the scenes of enthusiasm in the

stadium, nor Leoni's second relentless sprint ahead of dangerous little Pasotti, ahead of Pezzi, Tonini and the others; at this moment we are still unable to understand the new situation in the general classification that sees Leoni in the lead with an advantage of 4:43 over second-place Fazio, and about ten minutes over Coppi and eleven minutes over Bartali—won't such a gap begin to weigh against the two aces? And are they really so sure they can, in a twinkling of the eye, cut that to nothing on the alpine climbs? All that the mind retains of today's events is the image of a jubilant city on the seashore, full of sun, flags, happiness, bitter anguish, tears and laughter, an entire city that roared "Hurrah for Bartali, hurrah for Coppi," shouted almost with despair: "Hurrah for the Giro, hurrah for Cottur, hurrah for Doni," and wanted to say something quite different.

16

TODAY, A GREAT BATTLE
ON THE CLIMBS AND DESCENTS
OF THE DOLOMITES

Bassano del Grappa, the night of June 1

U GLY WEATHER. THIS EVENING, IN THE HOTELS and small inns—while big, ominous clouds continue to pile up to the north, toward the wall of the Dolomites—no one talks about the last stage that brought us one hundred and fifty kilometers from Udine, as far as the base of Monte Grappa. They only talk about tomorrow. This Thursday, June 2, the holy day of Sant'Erasmo Vescovo, will be the day of decision, the time of the Bogeyman, of the most difficult exami-  nation where the advice of one's companions, the easy knowledge of crib sheets, the formulas copied on fingernails and shirt-cuffs will not be worth a damn. The mountains will not permit themselves to be misled. They stand solemn and impenetrable, wrapped in an immense blanket of thick clouds, hiding destiny within themselves. Big words, these, which should only be used for wars, revolutions, tragedies and not for minor details of life like the Giro d'Italia.... But here in Bassano this evening the Giro is anything but a minor detail; it's the most important thing in life, by far, in the small world in which we are the wandering citizens. And the climb into the Dolomites keeps our senses on tenterhooks more or less as did the wait for the Anglo-American landing in France during the last war.

The stage today, while only short and raced on the flat, is not to be sneezed at. It was hard-fought (not by the great champions, of course, who continued to prevaricate). Even though the rain was pouring down—no more pleasant prospects of fields in the sunshine, bare-armed girls; no more steady fights with buckets of water set out on the road-sides, but an endless array of shiny umbrellas, slippery asphalt, and this ridiculous transformation of the cyclists in their little waterproof tunics that the wind billows out, form-ing monstrous hunchbacks—it was a continuous series of breaks. It began right at the gates of Udine: De Santis took off all by himself, his intentions not exactly clear. Also breaking away from the group, Soldani, Frosini and Franchi flew after him, but they couldn't keep it up. Then it was the turn of Frosini, this time with Ricci, Casola and three others; and this time they made it. They caught up with De Santi at Pordenone, but only after he had pocketed the prime.

Everyone was back together, again, coming into Treviso. But in Treviso, there was another escape. Doni, in the lead under the intermediate sprint banner, took advan-tage of the opportunity to step hard on the gas. After him went Corrieri, Schaer, and then Fornara. On a curve, Schaer ended up in the crowd. So only three were left. And in the gusting wind and rain, the trio pedaled for all they were worth between two dense lines of raincoats, oilskin capes and umbrellas that were almost unbroken, even in the open countryside. After Montebelluna, as if there were no more asphalt, the wheels started to throw up streams of mud. Corrieri tried to accelerate. He looked back. He saw that the other two were weakening. So there he was, dashing off toward the Bassano finishing line without any annoying escorts. "Bartali, Bartali!" people shouted on seeing the yellow jersey coming forward. "Bartali!" they continued to yell even when the fugitive was upon them. Who could have guessed that it was actually Corrieri? The mud had covered his face like a grotesque mask; it brought to mind one of those African witch doctors whose face was all tattooed in white. Recognition came only from behind when people could read his number. That was how Corrieri won the stage with more than a minute's lead (there was no change, however, in the overall classification).

A splendid stage, however, despite the rain and the mud. And yet it has already been stored away in the archives. And it appears that the preceding stages have also been relegated to the archives. The wise ones, the old foxes, the oracles, the professors, the astrologists, the chosen few who understand cycling esoterica, don't grant any importance to what has happened. In their opinion, the route covered until today, all 2296 kilometers of hardship, tribulations, sweat, suffering were nothing but a prologue. Therefore, the two great tenors have yet to test their scales (they haven't even cleared their throats—we should point out—not even a little trill, as a test). Up to now they have only been fencing with very slender foils. Tomorrow, at last, the warriors will grasp their broadsword with both hands, and down will come the blows full force. What does it matter if the first onslaught resulted in just a few superficial nicks here and there in the knights' skin? In one thrust tomorrow, the knight will slash his laughable opponents into pieces. What does it matter if Coppi and Bartali have a handicap of several minutes? Leoni is in surprisingly good shape and he dominates the sprints. But how will Leoni perform on the climbs? Yes, on the climbs? Tomorrow, snigger the experts, a ten-minute gap will be nothing. Up there, they say, only "the titans' powerful breath will reign supreme in the silence of the sheer valleys."

Glory is fragile even in cycling: A merest trifle is enough to turn the trumpets in another direction. We saw a little of that yesterday evening in Udine: contrary to expectations the cheers for the two champions were less sustained, and the crowd in front of their hotels was really sparse. Instead, the cheers and the crowd were concentrated under Leoni's windows. But the myth of Bartali and Coppi remains intact. It is touching—a heretic is speaking—the blind faith that sports enthusiasts have in those two.

What will happen tomorrow on the Rolle, Pordoi and Gardena passes? That is all they talk about during confabs secretly taking place within the teams, at the table during dinner, at the bar counter, from one bed to the other, in the dark, before sleep takes over. Rita Hayworth's wedding? Wychynski's obstructionism? The colonies? The Christian Democrats' congress? The day laborers' strike? You never hear talk of them. Rather, what will Bartali and Coppi do on the Pallidi peaks? In response to this question, a slightly ironic smile lights up the face of Pavesi, that wise old Silenus, who tutored both of them and knows more about cycling than Einstein knows about physics and the theory of relativity. He excludes only one thing: that the two will break away, taking turns at pulling. That would require, he says, that both Coppi and Bartali change into different men tonight. Excluding this eventuality, everything is possible: that Coppi attacks, beating his rival, that the contrary happens, or that the two, obsessed with watching one another, give up fighting. It is also possible, and we hope it will happen, that a young unknown will shake off the great aces like a great champion. And that roars will greet the revelation. And that beginning tomorrow a new name will echo throughout the world. But the professors shake their heads. It is absurd, they say. Bartali or Coppi, there can be no one else for the Dolomites.

Tonight, those peaks, arrogant and threatening, loom over the sleeping racers: visions of horrendous precipices, roads that make the blood run cold, without guardrails, and carved out of solid rock; and a monster follows them as they struggle up the slopes above the abyss, and salvation is up at the top, where there is a passage between the cliffs, where one never arrives. Even Fausto Coppi, even Gino Bartali, it's absolutely certain. They awake with a start, panting. They turn on the light. They look at their watch. They sigh. It's time to leave.

OPPOSITE PAGE
Wearing the 1949 Giro winner's pink jersey, Coppi was escorted from the finish to his open-doored team car. (Coppi is in the sunglasses.)

THIS PAGE
Corrieri won the Giro's final stage in a sprint at the Monza autodrome. After, Corrieri (left) celebrated with team leader Bartali (center) and their faithful teammate Jomaux (right).

17

IN A CLOSELY FOUGHT DUEL
AS THE STORM RAGES, COPPI
DEFEATS HIS MAIN ADVERSARY

Bolzano, the night of June 2

I T WAS UP THERE WHERE THE LINE OF FIR TREES was about to peter out—higher up were the bare meadows with traces of purplish-blue scree, the hotel already visible from the Passo di Rolle; still higher up the formidable pedestal of the Cimon della Pala immersed in a storm of dark clouds—that Bartali, who was leading the group, tried to break away. We saw him from above. He rocked in his saddle, shot ahead a few meters, and at the switchback's turn slowly looked back, show-

ing his sly, suspicious face. Were those behind him weakening? For several moments, out of the corner of his eye, he saw that the road immediately behind him had remained empty. At the same moment he felt the sudden warmth of the sun appearing between two black clouds. Then, all of a sudden, he had the sensation that a shadow was sticking to his back, one shadow, two, three, four following closely. He looked. Could there be the least doubt? It was Coppi. But he also saw Pasotti, Ronconi, Rossello, Cottur and Astrua.

Perhaps he mused: "He's holding on well, in the mountains, this little Pasotti! Still a bit fragile, to tell the truth, and rather young; but could he end up being my successor? And now? Should I persist? It's impossible that they will all stay wheel-to-wheel, after one thousand-eight hundred meters (6000 feet) of climbing. . . . But perhaps it is too soon? There's an awful lot of work to do today. Thank goodness I feel in control. This morning I was so nervous; that didn't used to happen to me."

He estimated the distance. There wasn't much ground to cover before the summit. Too late for an escape on the grand scale. He didn't insist. Nonetheless, he continued to ride in front, imperious, accelerating slowly. The peloton has collapsed. He hadn't made a mistake. He saw it in tatters scattering down the curves in the road. The wind. An ominous, sinister light on the glowing red edges of the Colibricon. The roar of the crowd waiting at the Passo di Rolle annoyed him. He heard them shouting his name. A King of the Mountain's sprint line: a one-minute bonus. He pushed down savagely on the pedals, he felt strong; another racer's bicycle wheel appeared alongside, trying to pull ahead of him. Piqued, three times he lifted himself out of the saddle, bringing all his weight down on the pedals. God, what a difficult road! Something that must have been a flower struck his face. The wheel beside him started to fall back. He crossed the sprint line in the lead, carried by the impetus of his burst, launched himself toward the valley, down the road to

Predazzo. Coppi faithfully followed him, as did the others, reunited in the little group. Except for Ronconi, who was seen at the foot of a fir tree, fussing with a wheel: a blow-out.

They found themselves together, hurtling down a vertiginous descent, on a gravelly road through a forest. And the forest had become dark. And the clouds were black in the extreme, all frayed underneath. Now and again, from the Dolomites, you'd catch sight through the mist of an occasional rugged rock. They felt something sting their faces and thighs. Hail. A storm in the mountains. Gradually, the scenery and the struggle grew impressively. The roadsides, the austere fir trees rushed away, all bent by the speed. Mud. The brakes squealed like kittens calling their mother. There wasn't a living soul. Nothing but the sound of the bicycles. The violent click-clock of the hail and the squeal of the brakes. Consequently, nothing was decided. At Predazzo, at the feed zone, there were many still in contention. Down there, at the bottom of the valley, the sun reappeared, no more hail nor wind; the racers were able to catch their breath.

Soon, the ordeal will begin again. But meanwhile, on the almost flat road, the big group reforms, almost a truce, one could say. The riders eat, drink, clean the mud from their faces; several are joking. Nerves relax a bit. Will the decisive challenge occur on the Pordoi?

Bartali peels a banana with his teeth. For just two seconds, he focuses on the fruit. When he lifts his eye again he sees three racers bursting clear. "They are breaking away!" he hears someone shout. He flings the banana away. He leans over, stretches his backside in that odd way of his, flattening himself on the bicycle. And he speeds away.

He doesn't need to ask who they are. Coppi's silhouette seen from any perspective is well-planted in his brain. Then there is the pink jersey, Leoni. And little Pasotti. They are moving at top speed. Luckily for him, Bartali has the excellent Jomaux, one of his lieutenants, with him. The others, Astrua, Rossello, Biagioni, Cecchi, Fornara, will certainly not give him any help.

Thus, it's practically on the flats, right where the danger seemed the least likely that the great duel, postponed from day to day, begins.

Bartali: to the devil with that damned banana. How is it possible that I let myself be taken by surprise like a child? Nothing other than a stupid blunder. And almost on the flat, where they fear me the least. "Come on, Jomaux! Move faster!" But Jomaux can do just so much. And Coppi draws away.

Bartali is readying himself to take the lead again (the sun has disappeared, but at the top end of the valley suddenly glistens the snow-streaked walls of the Sassolungo, like a fantastic cathedral at Christmastime), he is readying himself to take the lead when his rear tire suddenly goes flat. A wheel, quickly! His team car is ready, close by. Five, six, seven, ten seconds. Is it ready? Ready. Let's go! With Jomaux he catches back to the other pursuers, and takes command again. It takes more than that to scare him! Now the climb begins, that's his cup of tea. And he feels in fine fettle. Not the least concern. But how is it that Coppi and the other two have vanished? They are invisible as far as the eye can reach. Damn that moment of distraction!

Is it all the fault of a small distraction? Is it really that? Or is there something else as well? Look at him, Fausto

Coppi. Is he climbing? No, he is not climbing. He is simply racing, as if the road were as flat as a pool table. From a distance, one might say he was taking a merry spin. From a distance, that is: because close up one can see his face becoming more and more wrinkled and his upper lip drawn back, giving him the expression of a rat caught in a trap. And the two breakaway companions? Leoni is by now out-distanced, for the moment overcome by the pain. Pasotti, however, hangs on. Is this perhaps his first great day? Could he be the new star? Alas, one look at him is enough: a quiet, resigned air of suffering tightens his child-like face. It seems he can no longer see, so lackluster are his eyes. Ten more meters and Pasotti falls apart. Coppi is alone.

For a long moment, up to the Pordoi summit, then down to Arabba, and then up again to the Passo di Campolongo (another two hundred fifty meters—800 feet—up a very steep hill) and down again to the Plan Gardena crossroads, we follow him by car in his diabolical undertaking. He proceeds calmly, rising occasionally above the handlebars, harmoniously moving his tapering legs, solid at the upper joints, but slender at the calves. He does not turn to look back, he asks no advice from Tragella who, standing in the blue car, follows a few meters behind. He keeps going, going, under the fantastic Boè peak, livid and gloomy in that epic, stormy atmosphere, climbing among the thin pastures, always more alone. A racer on a bicycle, agreed. And us, for sure, we are not passionate fans. Yet there is something stirring about this slender young man who rides the mountains, one after the other, with nothing more than the beating of his heart. Downhill he does not force the pace, but matches the increasing speed with unneeded thrusts on the pedals; he tenses on the curves, then relaxes again as the road straightens out; methodical, always true to himself, his physical pain hermetically sealed within himself. Always more alone. No people in the fields, no motorcycle uproar, nor headlong avalanche of cars. In passing next to him, Verratti shouts: "Bravo, Coppi! You are five minutes ahead!" He lifts his head, moves his lips to say something, not a sound comes out. Yes, Bartali crossed the Pordoi five-and-a half minutes after him, preceded by Leoni and Pasotti.

And here we have reached the last torture, the Gardena Pass: another six hundred meters (2000 feet) to climb. Dismal crags loom up, ominous, as are the wild gorges from which wintry blasts of air descend. Coppi slows down a little. They are saying he has reached his limit. Finally we see him lift himself from the saddle, pedal three or four times, then recapture his former rhythm. His triumphant flight in the storm pauses. Odd rumors arrive with the motorcyclists who left Bartali a short while ago. Bartali has cut loose from the others and is pressing on alone. He has gained two minutes on the descent, they say. He is only now beginning to work full force. If Coppi weakens the slightest bit, the Other One will be right on his heels before the final summit.

By chance, on a curve, Coppi catches sight of his rival. Far away, it's true, awfully far below, still on the climb's first slopes. But he is making progress. How he stands out in the landscape, the yellow jersey of Gino Bartali, and the yellow car that escorts him! We stop to observe him, the man is striving with all his might. Actually, he is writhing on his saddle like a salamander surprised by a traveler in the middle of a trail. But it is not a sign of exhaustion. That's his style in difficult moments. And he alone, among all of the racers, keeps the exact same facial expression he had in Bassano this morning : cunning, sad, displeased, like certain ancient masks of the Medusa.

A feeling hard to describe, a kind of spiritual tension, pity, astonishment in the presence of this desperate duel, swept over the valleys. Would the old champion manage to save himself? Or was this the moment of destiny knocking? The blast of a horn reverberated, echoing from the peaks. It was the horn of a motorcycle messenger, yet it seemed to come from some solitary mountain god giving the signal. Then Coppi stopped swaying above the saddle; he had found a second wind, coming from some unknown source, the invisible hand of victory pulled him from place to place, and pushed him down the Val Gardena. He was flying now, terribly happy, though his face spoke only of pain.

He entered the Bolzano stadium, did the prescribed lap, and crossed the finish line. It was a triumph. And the empty minutes went by. One, two, three, five, six, seven…. A resounding roar finally announced that the Other One was arriving. He wasn't alone: the intrepid Leoni and young Astrua had managed to catch up with him on the final stretch. He did not appear to be tired. To the very last breath he battled for second place on the finishing straight—just like a soldier who fights a battle to the last even knowing it is lost. And then, separated by very long intervals, the others arrive. They all look crucified.

18

THE ROLE OF A LOSER
IS NOT FOR HIM

Bolzano, the night of June 3

T THIS POINT IN OUR STORY, IT WOULD HAVE been a good place to write a chapter on the great aging champion who finishes by giving up, and starting an irreversible decline. It would be so moving, and true to our sensibility that first rejoices for the winner and right afterward is moved by the drama of the defeated.... The outcome would be that much more effective because, in the present case, the man is no longer young, nor can he expect revenge in the near future;  the time available for him is now very limited. What has been, has been. This last frontier, beyond which hopes are forbidden, is not a vague myth on the other side of the horizon, but is very imminent, clearly visible, and far too convincing.

It would be so easy for someone writing about the Giro d'Italia to move the reader by insisting on such a bitter thing. Because nobody in the world is as deserving of pity as the man who from the height of glory crashes down day by day, without being at fault, until he finds himself back to where he started as a boy; when no one points him out on the street and, little by little, his name loses the magic that gave him his fame, and he reverts to being one of the countless names listed in the phone book.

It would be splendid to describe the champion who, immediately after the finish, shuts himself up in his hotel room and takes a shower, stripping off his coating of mud. But the warmth of the water, the soap, the immaculate freshness of the bed awaiting him (here in Bolzano especially, where the cleanliness and the art of making guests feel good reaches the highest level)—the thought of taking a day of rest, the newspapers newly arrived, the huge complimentary Milanese cake with its tricolor ribbon sent to him in homage—do not comfort him as usual. On the contrary, all that only aggravates the wound, reminding him of other showers, other beds, other evenings of rest during the golden years, when victory, as long as he really wanted it, became his. It is the moment when, in the streets, the enthusiasts who remained faithful to him call to him; and for the first time this evening he listens to them with avid interest; and he peeks out, desolately, between the slats of the white shutters: what faint voices, what a miserable little crowd compared to the roaring multitudes of the past! He hated them, then, with a kind of repugnance. Dear, simple, generous friends, where are you now?

And to present the scene at dinner: All the cyclists on the team are seated with the team manager, the masseur, the mechanics, et cetera, at the same long table. But this evening, the usual liveliness is missing. No one has the courage to be the first to speak, as happens in the house of a condemned person right after the sentence has been pronounced. It is he, the champion, who deliberately breaks the ice, uttering some unimportant words, without the slightest reference to what happened a few hours ago. As if it were just another evening, during a training period, for example, when it is hard to find a suitable topic for conversation at the table. But this strained indifference just increases the uneasiness. No one replies to his trite remarks. In the painful silence, his teammates keep their eyes glued to their plates, pretending to be extremely busy boning the chicken; one of them coughs. Only the waiters, motionless, a little to one side, stare hungrily at the defeated giant, with the indiscreet, obsessive curiosity aroused by great physical deformities.

Or the night, when the champion in decline wakes up, tormented by bad dreams. To find peace, he lights a cigarette: Bartali is one of the few racers who smoke, and he walks in circles around his room. Outside and inside the hotel, no one says a word, nobody is thinking about him at this moment; everyone has sunk into the black abyss of sleep and takes no heed of him. Think of the overwhelming sadness of this man surrounded by the ghosts of the past, and assess his present fate. From the corridor, from the rooms nearby, the sounds of the rhythmic snores of the others reach him; today, they are still his subjects but tomorrow, under his very eyes, they will throw themselves into breakaways; and he, for the first time, will try in vain to keep up with their irresistible pace. The young generation! They are snoring like animals, storing up more and more strength, like warriors working secretly at sharpening their swords, while he smokes and wastes his dwindling energy.

It would be fine and greatly to our advantage to insist on this fascinating theme. But this isn't the reality. In order to do so it would be necessary to turn the truth upside down. Because the champion of whom we speak is not someone defeated by life, he is not a romantic hero, not a pathetic figure betrayed by the inexorable march of time. But we are dealing with a strange being, tough, obstinate, in a certain sense not very human, quite unlike us, who does not recognize despondency, nor the depressing influence of adverse circumstances. He grumbles, complains, protests constantly, it is true; he does it, though, out of habit—even when things are going well. A rough, thorny stronghold in which there is no place for discouragement. He has been beaten. He knows it and does not look for excuses. But he is exactly the same as he was before. The idea of giving up does not even enter his mind. He feels in top form, neither more nor less than during the famous days of his career. So he is not sad, he does not have to play a part to show he is calm, he doesn't feel the slightest bit condemned.

Alfredo Binda, who led him to victory last year in the Tour de France and who yesterday followed the Dolomite stage to size up the situation in view of the upcoming Tour, told us that yesterday Bartali was riding as well as he had done last summer: but in France in 1948, Coppi was not there, that's the whole explanation.

The drama of physical decline is not yet something for him. It will emerge in the future because it is inevitable. But there's no question of speaking of that today. A chain of adverse circumstances hounded Bartali yesterday, maintains his team manager Vittorio Colombo. The rotten luck—he tells us—began right after Predazzo, when the racers were eating. It happened at the feed zone. Aware that his rear tire was slowly going flat, Bartali mentioned it to Jomaux, his lieutenant. Jomaux made the mistake of approaching his team car, shouting the news at the top of his lungs. Coppi heard it and since, Colombo says, he is the cleverest racer who ever existed, he took advantage of the opportunity. Thus, the attack. Meanwhile, Bartali, the eternal malcontent that he is, wasted precious time arguing with Colombo whether to change the wheel right away and then about the gear ratio of the wheel itself. Launching himself in pursuit at last, Bartali forgot to eat. And, when you race, food is like coal for a boiler. At a certain point, therefore, he found himself short of energy, and down the Gardena Pass toward Ortisei and Bolzano his progress was quite bad, his pace frightfully slow, especially for a fast descender like him.

This is what Colombo said. They are explanations that could almost sound like excuses. This was certainly not said by Bartali who, if he loses, knows to take his punishment without accusing anyone, nor does he torment himself regretting what could have been and instead was not. Where, then, is the figure who would have served us so well for the most moving chapter of our story? How can one feel pity for a loser who does not feel defeated? Or a poor devil who's not fazed by his bad luck? Or a relatively old man to whom the misery of old age is unknown? Therefore, last night, Bartali found the same consolation in the shower and at the dinner table as the other days. At the table, he did not feel the need to feign a false serenity, and he grumbled as usual. And he did not wake in the middle of the night to mull things over; Indeed, he slept right through the night until nine this morning.

So don't cry for the defeated champion quite yet. Do not feel sorry for him; do not make of him a hero in decline; do not send sympathy messages. He doesn't need them. And if any one of you suffering the pains of old age thinks you can be consoled by a comparison with Bartali, you are mistaken. Mr. Gino Bartali is not old, nor is he discouraged or sad. And he is too sure of himself to offer excuses. This morning someone said to him: "Tell me, did you puncture two or three times?" He replied: "Punctured? We never puncture."

19

THE "GREAT ONES" DON'T FLINCH
WHEN THE "LESSER MEN" BREAK AWAY

Modena, June 4

MAGINE THE ROAD FROM BOLZANO, LEADING TO the plains at Verona, on a magnificent morning, with the caravan of the Giro d'Italia revitalized by an entire day of rest. One has to climb a good way up the mountains in order to be able to see all of it. Here is the pacesetting vehicle: an, armor-plated Jeep, shaped like an ice-cream van, with four journalists on board. Our beefy colleague Slawitz, head of this little group, woke up late and now he is hurrying ahead in search of the breakfast he had to skip in Bolzano due to his hasty departure. The Jeep takes off and we enjoy a minute of silence until the appearance of the real avant-garde: The cars belonging to the press and radio stations, fitted with odd antennas resembling those of insects, more cars of the organization, the race jury, the time-keepers; and

in among these a noisy confusion of motorcycles: reporters, messengers, photographers, couriers and the tireless Milanese traffic policemen; not to mention the very popular Corsi, a giant with the heart of a child, everybody's brotherly friend, as completely happy as a bird in springtime, who is performing a few acrobatic leaps with his motorcycle for the benefit of the citizens lined up along the road. We see uniforms of every style: big, fur-lined jackets; cowboy shirts; swimsuits; crash helmets; red, American-style caps; big, pirate-like neckerchiefs. Sober family men take advantage of the Giro to display the most insane, clownish coquetries they wouldn't dare dream of at home. A few minutes later the main group appears: first, a squad of traffic policemen, and right behind them, the racers, a multicolored swarm that from a distance glows and sparkles like a carnival. Immediately following, the little red flag in his right hand, is Giuseppe Ambrosini, the dynamic race director. Then come the various team cars, each one the colors of their respective racers' jerseys, bristling with racks carrying spare wheels and bicycles. More press cars, more motorcycles, repair trucks, more loudspeaker vans on which are mounted huge speakers blasting out news and ditties. At the tail end of the peloton we see struggling—but there is no need, the speed today is so slow—a rider left behind by a flat tire, but we are too far away to make out who he is. Finally come two rearguard motorcyclists and an untidy wake of fans in cars, on motorcycles and bicycles, proud to breathe the air that moments before had entered the lungs of Coppi, Bartali and Leoni.

It is a fine sight, the Giro's caravan, so young and happy. And it inspires faith in life. This morning it made its appearance in perfect order, well-combed, newly shaven, blooming like an athlete after his bath. And it doesn't seem to be in a hurry.

We come down from the mountains and move forward with the first cars in the procession. We do not exceed twenty-seven kilometers an hour. The sun invites us to have a little nap. But all of a sudden a car—its logo is that of a well-known newspaper—passes us at an insane speed. Why? What has happened? Has someone broken away from the peloton and is right on our heels? Should we race ahead to avoid being caught in a traffic jam? Nobody knows anything, but the mere sight of that car sets off the alarm. An illogical hysteria sweeps over the drivers and motorcyclists. Another car shoots off after the first one, and then a third, siren howling, tries to get ahead of them. We feel as though we are on the race track at Indianapolis. An awful bellowing of car horns resounds in the valley, the speedometer wavers: one hundred an hour; very soon the caravan has stretched itself over a dozen kilometers. At last the lead car is all alone, lost at the edge of the Adige River. Looking back, not a living soul is visible. We stop. Silence. Sparrows chirping. A minute goes by, two, five and finally the others start showing up. What had happened? Nothing, absolutely nothing. The riders are still all together, moving at the pace of a spring promenade. We are again gliding along very slowly, and go back to dozing, when, all of a sudden, a motorcyclist rushes by waving his right hand furiously, as if he were announcing an enemy attack. What is happening? Nobody knows anything at all. Tension rages again. We think we hear Leoni's name when a colleague leans out of his car shouting something indistinctly. "Did Leoni break away?" we ask. "Oh, yes? Did Leoni break away?" he replies, not having understood us. And away we go at a mad speed. And the others follow. And once again a chaotic "much ado about nothing." Until we are again far away in the silent valley, absolutely alone. So we stop. What had happened? Nothing. The riders are still all in a group, still moving at a snail's pace.

This was repeated four or five times as we drove through the valley, but absolutely nothing happened among the racers; nerves were constantly strained; the conflict between the two super-champions, even more dramatic after the Dolomites, was like an inflamed lymph gland about to flare up, there, in the calm group; and from one moment to the other, it could explode, even though the completely flat road wasn't favorable for battles. At each excited shout, at each motorcyclist's gesture, at the least sign of anything that could somehow cause alarm, pandemonium broke out again: ten minutes of superfluous fever that subsided into the lethargic rhythm of before. And during this time, as we gradually moved to the south, the sun became brighter, the houses less peaked, the surrounding mountains huddled increasingly lower, the Adige became more austere, fewer and fewer men wore blue aprons, the cliffs were less often crowned by ancient castles, the trees became more stately, and the girls less and less fair-haired.

"Hey, are these racers sleeping?" the boys who had already been waiting several hours asked us. Not actually asleep, but you could easily believe it. Just before Rovereto, a breakaway attempt by Carollo was quickly quashed: two, three riders caught up with him, placed themselves on either side, and wedging him with their elbows, politely led him to the back. The following small attacks had no effect other than to get the cars in the retinue all worked up for nothing.

And so? A stage without a story? Just about. The history of cycling will certainly not remember Bevilacqua (today in extraordinarily good form) taking the intermediate sprint at Verona, ahead of Conte and Leoni. Nor—at the risk of seeming cruel—the breakaway before Ostiglia by Barducci and Drei, that was quickly caught by Bevilacqua and then six others, to wit, Conte, Carrea, Logli, Seghezzi, Pezzi and Tonini. It was foreseeable. And since none of the nine could upset the overall classification, the others displayed their tolerance.

The arrival of the runaways in Modena, Conte's victory and the gap to the "great ones" are recorded in detail in the proper order on page 187. We should mention the rest here: unequaled sunshine, entire populations packed along the roadside and almost out of their minds with enthusiasm, a sort of apotheosis at the overflowing stadium, and the extreme difficulty to concentrate for those of us who are writing because of the uproar of the crowd in the street: Unluckily, and how it happened is unknown, the news that Fausto Coppi is staying at our hotel has become public knowledge.

20

LEONI OUTSPRINTS COPPI ON MONTECATINI'S HIPPODROME

Montecatini, the morning of June 6
[Ciro Verratti]

ESTERDAY, THE PINK JERSEY HELD FIRM BY A light puff of air, the puff of air that was the final sprint on the long, heavy horse-race track in Montecatini. If Coppi had arrived first, the symbolic pink garment would have changed masters; but Leoni, feeling the jersey to which he had become so attached slipping off his shoulders, called on all his talent as the greyhound sprinter and, in that moment, thrust his wheel ahead of our exceptional racer in the white-and-sky-  blue jersey. Nothing new, then, in this Giro, since if Coppi gained fifteen seconds on the Abetone and thirty seconds at the finish, in compensation Leoni added a full minute to his overall lead and, even if it were by so little, strengthened his position. He still has a few days' breathing space and, by all appearances, the Giro d'Italia is still alive.

Of course, if Leoni wins the mountain stage, it would

mean there was no battle in the mountains: This is one of the self-evident truths of Italian cycling. This time, Coppi was probably merciful, but it also has to be said that Leoni, with that jersey on his back, has become a titan and he defends it with a passion and, above all, with a tenacity that until now was not thought to be a part of his champion's repertoire. In truth, this is something new for him, since, as he says himself, despite his class he has spent his life being a *gregario*, even if it was as the teammate of great captains. First he was Coppi's squire, then Bartali's, and he always had to bow to the will, not to say the whims, of the masters. Now, he has finally freed himself of slavery and has started to work for himself, to be, as he says, "his own *gregario*." He's living in a new world, where the responsibilities are greater, but the satisfactions even more far-reaching, a world in which he lives to the full, and that he likes enormously.

Everything we saw on this stage has been practically erased from our memory to make room for what we saw on arriving at the Abetone pass. There, Tuscany came to meet us and it was a suffocating, merciless meeting. Think what Tuscany means in cycling and realize that it had to vent all its passion on the only stage the Giro granted it this year. It had to liquidate all of its unlimited reserves of cycling fervor at one time. Here in Montecatini's vast square, under our windows when we arrived, there was the most colossal traffic jam we have ever seen in our lives. Only God knows how we managed to get out of it, since there were no police and everything was left to the initiative, ability and goodwill of each individual. In Italy, the individual initiative works miracles, but here discipline and common sense were completely overcome by the desire to see Bartali, a desire that is profound in all of Italy, but in Tuscany it reaches a worrisome level that could result in the most unpredictable consequences. Furthermore, this is a region where all the pillars of our cycling culture collapse. In all the other places, Coppi and Bartali are the columns supporting the structure, the two fixed stars around which all the others rotate like small planets, satellites and comets. Here in Tuscany you go into one district where a single idol reigns, and it is Soldani; in another, people rave about Cecchi; in still another, Biagini captures all hearts. Because Tuscany gave birth to a good half of the Italian racers, and each of them has his own little fief here. Towering above everyone else, of course, is Bartali, the despot, who is even more cantankerous and inflexible in Tuscany than elsewhere, and who is perhaps so much loved precisely for this reason. They pretend to ignore Coppi: The expressions of enthusiasm for him are isolated and almost always of outside origin. They cannot forgive him for having dimmed Bartali's glory, and that's why we think that if a Tuscan were caught shouting "Hurrah for Coppi" he would be considered a traitor.

When we left Modena, the crowd's greatest interest was not in the pink jersey, Leoni, nor in Coppi and Bartali, but in Carollo, to wit, the "black jersey." Our jolly accomplices from the *giringiro* (the Giro's racers) have created a new symbolic jersey: that for the last racer in the overall classification, who for this unwelcome privilege picks up a slew of prizes in addition to a hefty daily gratuity. You know what it's like here on earth: people are always moved by the sight of the destitute or those who are mistaken for one, and they loosen their purse strings right away. Who in this caravan of athletes is the weakest? Who in this realm of the powerful is the most obscure? There he is! They've identified him; it's the black jersey, to whom all hearts reach out. Little by little, a situation is evolving that makes the black jersey more profitable than the pink one, and those who find themselves at the tail end of the overall classification are beginning to exercise all their skill and ingenuity to win it, taking care, naturally, not to violate the "maximum time" rule. The truth is, if Leoni's pink jersey is somewhat insecure, Carollo's black jersey is firmly attached to its holder by invisible, but quite solid ties. It is a matter that is beginning to worry the race director because there is a whole group of *gregari* tempted to race to lose and they look at the overall classification with unnatural desires. It came into being as a joke, but it is becoming something serious.

The first kilometers were without incident, and the peloton's peaceful intentions were clear as we slowly neared the first climb of the day, the one leading to Pavullo. A gentle slope that takes you higher almost without your being aware of it, and since no one had given the slightest sign of aggression, the first fifty kilometers were absolutely uneventful. After Pavullo, the road becomes dusty and takes on the typical mountain characteristics: the turns are more frequent and narrower, the grade is pretty steep in places. On this hill, Leoni is hit by his second flat tire of the day, having had the first after eighteen kilometers, without consequences. The pink jersey having stopped, the peloton quickly broke up, and at the front Coppi, Bartali and Astrua formed a small patrol. It could have been the start of a decisive break, since the two aces were there, but it's clear that the top climbers have no wish to work hard; and so Leoni, at the head of a spirited chase group, rejoined them before the Barigazzo summit at an elevation of twelve-hundred twenty-one meters (4006 feet); there, about thirty racers crossed in a compact group. On the descent, minor dramas due to flat tires victimized Pasotti, Maggini, Fondelli, Ottusi and Milano. By the foot of the climb leading to Abetone they have already caught up with the others and, with the exception of the habitual backmarkers, everyone is there: at least fifty riders.

The Abetone climb, which is the highest col the Giro will cross in the Apennines, is the day's disappointment. Riding ahead of the racers, we get stiff necks looking back to see when Bartali or Coppi will launch their attack, but this attack never materializes, so we reach the summit recording in our notebooks the climbers' refusal to do battle. Here, hundreds of cars and buses have unloaded one of the densest crowds of cycling fans ever gathered for the Giro d'Italia. For at least two kilometers we pass through a narrow corridor of swaying spectators, among whom we saw many who seemed to be downright crazed. The roar of "Bartali, Bartali" reverberated from tens of thousands of chests, but instead of Bartali or Coppi, it's Pasotti who passes first under the mountain prize banner; Bartali and Coppi have to be satisfied with second and third place. All the others arrive almost wheel-to-wheel, with Leoni twenty seconds behind. A bit of a disappointment for a crowd that had perhaps dreamed of a historical climb and a new, exciting battle between the giants, probably ending with Bartali's resounding revenge over his passionately hated rival. So it was clear that they took no pleasure to see this sight.

On the descent, it's Pasotti who goes on the attack, dropping everyone. We watch him launch himself toward the plain at breakneck speed, throwing caution to the wind, on the way, perhaps, to achieving a resounding victory; but unfortunately the impetuous young man's dream is short-lived. A flat tire awaits him halfway to his goal and when we see him put one foot on the ground, two big tears streak down his cheeks. He is just one of those who has no luck, the very incarnation of unrewarded courage. But he is not the only one to puncture; many others keep him company, including Corrieri, Drei, Cerami, Pedroni, Missine, Milano and Jomaux. However, the mishaps are not finished because a little further ahead a mass pileup puts about ten racers on the ground, including Bartali, Biagini, Schaer and Simonini. We're not about to forget the despair of those spectators who saw Bartali fall: from one valley to the next the disastrous news has spread all over Tuscany, and from that moment on, they talked about nothing else. But it was just a trifle, as the riders picked themselves up and carried on.

At the gates of Pistoia, we see Soldani break away and arrive triumphantly in his city, but he is caught in short order, as his break was no more than a gesture for his fellow citizens. Coming into Montecatini, Maggini, Astrua and Fondelli take a fall on a dusty stretch of road, and finally it's a dense group that enters the hippodrome where, as we told you, Leoni saves his pink jersey at the moment of Coppi's attack. A splendid, long final sprint, rich in emotion, at the end of which Bartali was carried in triumph.

This morning at 9:45 we will leave for Genoa. The Giro makes its entry into the enchanted scenery of the Riviera.

21

THE LIGURIAN AIR, WHICH THRIVES IN THEIR BACKYARD, GIVES WINGS TO THE ROSSELLO BROTHERS

Genoa, the night of June 6

HERE ARE THE MOST NOTABLE CHARACTERS OF the fourteenth stage—228 kilometers in bright sunshine, by mountains and valleys, alongside the sea: a succession of turns, not by a road, but a human corridor almost without a break (the giants again did not commit themselves today; so that out of fourteen stages, one can say that only one, the one in the Dolomites, was fought tooth and nail; this is certainly distressing for those who naïvely would like the super  champions to do battle every hour of the race, but there can't be a solution to that until some new rival emerges). So here they are:

Vincenzo and Vittorio Rossello of Savona, first and third, respectively, at the Genoa finishing line (Pedroni was second), with a two-minute gap over the peloton. Native air—that's a law that you very often confirm—gives racers extraordinary energy. As soon as they approach their town or village, and from one place and another they start to hear echoes of their local dialect, so familiar to them, then even the nags, the last-of-the-line *gregari*, those relegated to the bottom of the overall classification, are transformed into lions. The old Latin proverb that says, "No man is a prophet in his own country," is not applicable to cycling. On the contrary…. If you want to be loved by your fellow villagers, become a bike racer. Then, in your own neighborhood—whatever your success—they will consider you a Girardengo[10]. And this affection is a source of great pride; even the most wretched manage for a few minutes to vie with Coppi. At the very least, when the local rider cannot count on very strong legs, he will make a break near his hometown; posters singing his praises hang from telephone poles and balconies, his name is written in huge letters on the asphalt, along with those of the "great ones." The people recognize him immediately, not needing to decipher his number. It is like an appointment looked forward to with pleasure for many days. Waiting for him there are his mother; his fiancée with a little basket of rose petals; his former schoolmaster who taught him his A-B-Cs and put on his black suit in honor of the occasion; the priest who baptized him; the young girl who gave him his first kiss; his childhood friends, with whom he made his first bike rides (it was a rickety, heavy contraption, so high that his foot never reached the bottom of the pedal stroke); there is his manager, the president of the local

---

10. Constante Girardengo was the first Italian "campionissimo." He won the Giro d'Italia twice (1919 and 1923), Milan-San Remo six times, and the Tour of Lombardy three times.

Salus et robur[11] club, who bought him his first real racing bike; the policeman who fined him for speeding; the town beauty queen who never tired of teasing him; friendly strangers, but also enemies from his own town, all lined up: any ill feelings are forgotten and everybody yells his name. What does it matter if ten kilometers up the road, where no one knows him, the poor racer falls apart, and if this evening he has a hard time making it within the time limit? Isn't it all worth it? Isn't it stupendous to come through all alone, yes, ahead of Leoni and Bartali like a triumphant hero?

In the more fortunate cases, the fugitive hopes to win a prime. And in the most favorable of all cases—but one has to know how to do it—it is actually winning the stage that he has his heart set on.

Down in Sicily, we saw Fazio drop everyone and win in Catania; we saw Bevilacqua and De Santi shoot ahead of everyone under the banners held up in their respective hometowns in the Veneto; Tonini in Emilia; Soldani in Pistoia's hills yesterday. Today, it's the two likeable Rossello brothers who, to be honest, are anything but second-raters, and it can be said their name always resounds when some boisterous activity is going on. They shot off with Pedroni on the descent to Recco, and stepped on the gas, to take two minutes out of the giants; never have we seen two such happy boys arrive at the finish line. But if they had wanted to—a malicious person might ask—couldn't the giants have overtaken them? Weren't they being kind-hearted and under-standingly lenient? And even if that were so, we reply, what

11. Latin for "energy and health."

does it matter? The Rossello brothers did a great race, and their compatriots, on seeing them arrive in the lead, seemed to have gone crazy. What more can one ask?

Alfredo Pasotti from Pavia, twenty-three years old, winner of the mountain prize on the Bracco (yesterday on the Abetone). He is perhaps the most graceful racer. Not movie-star handsome like Leoni, but he is well proportioned, slender, his face still that of an adolescent, his manner courteous, and in the saddle he has a well-balanced style. If he were not so slim and delicate he probably would already be a great champion. Since the elimination from the race of Casola—the eccentric Casola—for being outside the time limit, Pasotti is his team's leader. On the Pordoi's slopes, he was the last to be dropped by Coppi. All the others had already been left behind in the valley, and still he resisted. We passed closely by him at the moment of his crisis. His face ashen, he looked at us with the aggrieved expression of one who is being wronged; but he was resigned to it. He was soon left behind. A classic case of blowing up. He had probably expected too much of himself and, obsessed with the idea of keeping up with Coppi, he had forgotten to eat. At the Pordoi summit, he passed second. Then he caved in completely. Yesterday as well, descending the Abetone, we saw him in total crisis. Suddenly, and we weren't expecting it because our car was flying along, a racer passed us at a crazy speed. Number 86: Pasotti. We looked behind us. No one else was in sight. Like a downhill racer concentrating totally on an acrobatic ski jump, we saw him, light and delicate, disappear in front of us. To try to follow him closely by car would have been madness. But just after the next turn we saw him again: He was off his bike and tearing off—that's the exact expression—the front wheel of his bicycle in his haste to change the tire. His tire had gone flat for the second time. He looked around himself, searching for his team's car that would give him a spare wheel. But the car wasn't there. The tears were running down his face, tracing tiny, thin, crooked grooves in the mud encrusting it.

Serse Coppi, twenty-five years old, Fausto's brother, took third place in the Chiavari intermediate sprint. It's the first time in this Giro that his name is mentioned—even so modestly—in newspaper reports. We certainly do not claim here to discover him. Many have spoken and written about him…. Who is not familiar with this unique, and in certain ways pathetic, counterpart of the great champion, a "double" who has the same face, blood and name but, in athletic terms, can almost look like an ironic imitation? Who doesn't know of the exemplary affection between the two brothers, which is not compromised in any way by their enormous difference in class? Serse not only feels no envy, he rejoices in Fausto's victories even more than Fausto himself; Fausto cannot do without Serse and feels lost if he doesn't know that behind him, in the group of backmarkers, Serse is slogging away faithfully. The technicians say that Serse, while not lacking in quality, is the only cyclist in the world who doesn't know how to ride a bicycle. His style—and even we laymen notice it—is disconcerting; some compare him to a duck, others to a giraffe, still others to an accordion. If he didn't sway his hips at each pedal stroke, they say, he could do a lot better. But it seems there's no remedy for that. His face is just like his brother's, minus that clever expression, but with the addition of a pair of very gentle, kind eyes. He is often mistaken for Fausto and this heightens the emotional tension created by this situation. At the end of one stage, we ourselves saw an austere gentleman about fifty years old approach him and offer him a huge bouquet of roses, stammering confused, congratulatory phrases. "But, you know...." said Serse, highly embarrassed. "Oh, allow me!" the admirer begged. And Serse, with a sad, cherubic smile: "But, you know.... Me, I'm his brother!"

Doesn't it seem like the subject of a sentimental play, this shared life of two such different brothers, one indifferent to glory, the other heedless of mediocrity and bad luck? (Because Serse's terrible crash in the Giro two years ago near Terontola was surely misfortune, as was the annulment of his only big victory, in the last Paris-Roubaix.) In the world of Italian cycling this is perhaps the most touted topic when the object is to arouse the public's sympathy. But is all this true, after all? Does Serse deserve so much compassion? We have become somewhat doubtful. Perhaps what we mean to say is that the roles simply ought to be reversed. On the basis of many small signs we believe we have discovered the most recent truth about the Giro...a very surprising truth.

Serse—that's the fascinating hypothesis—is Fausto's lucky charm, his guardian spirit, a sort of living talisman—a little like the magic lamp without which Aladdin would have remained forever a beggar. Who knows, perhaps in Serse lies the entire secret of his champion brother. If Serse were to give up cycling, perhaps the enchantment would dissipate and Fausto would suddenly find himself without strength, like a limp rag. Partners, then: They are so closely tied that neither is capable of living without the other. It is Serse who really wins, because without him Fausto would have fallen apart a hundred times. Serse is the deserving one, and that's sufficient reward for him. This helps him to withstand terrible efforts (certain that he'll finish among the last riders), to put up with humiliating comparisons, to not get angry when he is mistaken for Fausto and is offered flowers that are not meant for him. But of course, Serse is worthy of all this generosity, even if you think that our hypothesis is a fairy tale. Look at him, with that nice-guy face, those two big gentle eyes, so understanding they seem to be hiding something....

Another person figuring in the stage, mentioned last only as a matter of chronology, is an officer of Celere Genoa's flying squad—who I can't identify better than that—due to whose intervention one of the Giro's finest stages ended in a regrettable scene. This officer is a tall fellow, about thirty, with a sharp, somewhat bird-like face, and thin Mongol-like mustache. Assigned to maintain order at the Lido d'Albaro finishing line, for no apparent reason he charged in his Jeep a group of journalists, team managers and race judges, who had just got out of their cars and had gathered at the finishing line as they have always done and always do, without causing the slightest inconvenience. We, too, were there and, flabbergasted, saw the officer (who we assume thought the journalists were intruders), yelling and twirling his black rubber truncheon, rain down blows on the nearest heads. Our colleague Giuseppe Ambrosini, the race director, was standing right below the jury rostrum. The officer dealt him a fierce blow right on his forehead, lacerating the skin. As the vehicle inched forward, he went after several others. Many of our colleagues were beaten in this way, among them our Ciro Verratti and Guido Giardini, who lost his watch in the incident. A senseless excess of individual zeal? Or did the officer really suffer mental breakdown? The local police chief, who came rushing to the scene, fully understood the anger it aroused throughout the Giro's entourage. And shortly afterward the mayor sent Emilio De Martino, director of the *La Gazzetta dello Sport*, a letter stating how very sorry Genoa's citizens and all its sports enthusiasts were about what had happened.

In Genoa, an immense, festive crowd had turned out to welcome the Giro. It had been a day of sunshine, amid stupendous countryside and an admirable crowd, and it ended stupidly.

22

LITTLE PASOTTI IS MUCH TOO ALONE

San Remo, the night of June 7

ODAY THE SEA: FLOWERS (A WATERFALL OF carnations and roses rained down on the caravan from garden railings), grade crossings (from Pegli to Savona a pesky local train regularly blocked the crossings, and as the racers managed to pass under the barrier but not the cars, the result was a series of disturbing pursuits protected from on high by the merciful God of the Giro), then the amaryllis, broom and all those magnificent ornamental plants whose names we  have never been able to learn. Furthermore, as usual, crowds of spectators, but of a different kind: people, that is to say, who were mostly on vacation, accustomed to living peacefully and who had certainly not woken up before ten o'clock; half-naked young girls, and already, well-tanned, in their sundresses, lifeguards in their brand new uniforms, convalescents in pajamas, kids from the holiday camps wearing their large, white cloth hats; and here and there we spotted a few Scandinavian poetesses who looked at us with disgust. And, at Cogoleto, Mr. Antonio Buelli's brass band playing music.

Every time the Giro passes through Cogoleto the band strikes up a little quasi-triumphal march.

The Cogoleto band is like a monument in honor of bicycle racing. Look at the instruments: each one has a copper-plate label bearing an inscription "Giro d'Italia 1919," "Giro di Lombardia 1921," "Milano-Sanremo 1922," and so on. And if each one had a voice in addition to its sound, its narratives would continue evening after evening. Now Antonio Buelli manages a restaurant and he doesn't complain. But at that time—and we must go back to the deep abyss of the past, that is, as far as the fabulous days of Girardengo—Buelli, then a bicycle racer, had trouble making ends meet. Passion for cycling, he had, even too much of it; his legs were his despair. Imagine a Malabrocca thirty years ago, though without Malabrocca's picaresque glory, coming to the forefront because of his position as last in the overall classification (now, however, Carollo has stolen the title from him by a margin, negative, of course, that is almost too wide to be bridged; and he firmly intends to hold on to it because ownership of the black jersey, which does not really exist, confers on the holder, besides a pleasant popularity, all of ten thousand lire a day offered by tender-hearted sponsors). But in those days the last place did not equate with cash; no one was interested in it and Buelli, who almost always found himself at the back, did not attain any glory from it.

The fact is that Buelli, realizing that winning races was not exactly his vocation, fell back on his second and, until then, secret ambition: music. He continued to pedal, resigned to swallowing the dust left in the wake of the aces, but no longer with any hope of success. To establish a brass band in Cogoleto, his hometown, became his new purpose in life. And by pedaling, pedaling—every so often an unexpected sprint or the goodwill of the champions made it possible for him to win a few meager primes in small towns—the music lover put away some cash on the side. By dint of racing, struggling and sweating, he was able one fine day to lay the cornerstone of the great monument: He bought a drum. So, when the first race came through this district, the racers (and he, too, was among them) were welcomed to Cogoleto by an enthusiastic drumroll, like those at the circus announcing that the trapeze artists were about to perform their death-defying triple leap. In front of the lines of people stood a man, adequately trained by Buelli himself, wearing a braid-trimmed cap, and beating, beating on his donkey skin with the rhythm of a virtuoso. The great band ensemble was born.

And he still raced, the brave Buelli, always intent on achieving that second objective of his. From a Giro d'Italia came the first cornet, and from a series of track meets the first trumpet. And meanwhile the years went by, and the legs that had never been, to tell the truth, great legs, were getting heavier. Six, seven band players now were waiting for the caravan—an impressive group, especially for the volume of their sound, compared to the original drum. But it was not yet the authentic, complete band that Buelli wanted.

By sweating and making economics, finally the dream

became a reality. And one day, Buelli appeared in person on the street to welcome the Giro's racers; wearing a richly braided cap and, holding a baton in his hand, he led at least sixteen musicians lined up with all the instruments required by a band worthy to be so called. The maestro lifted his right arm very high and, with a dictatorial gesture, gave the go-ahead for the trumpets' blare. Happy? Yes, the great project had been achieved. Cogoleto possessed a real band ensemble for which the envious neighboring towns would eat their hearts out, and it was all thanks to him. He had not lived in vain after all. But at the same time he considered all the years he had used up; he saw his already-worn face reflected in the very shiny side of the trombone; he thought about his bicycle gathering dust in a closet, its tires flat and twisted; and he heard the voices of the champions greeting him. The champions, spurred on by their youth, moved away at top speed along the big highway. And instead he had to remain there in Cogoleto, his four walls, henceforth immobile, forever.

Buelli was in his usual place today, too, faithfully keeping this sentimental rendezvous, with his splendid band. In truth, very few of the racers knew who he was. Hardly anyone shouted a greeting to him. Nevertheless, we had never heard music so strongly permeated, so to speak, with the spirit of cycling's epic deeds: it spoke of the entire golden era, the mad dashes on the tracks, a gasping ordeal climbing the Alps, Ganna's and Galetti's legendary break-aways, the velodromes thundering with applause, the memories, the nostalgia, together with the premonition of the most improbable victories. It would have taken a lot more to move the old-timers, who were by now skeptical and completely without illusions. However, the notes penetrated the hearts of the youngest, who pricked up their ears and were suddenly convinced that fate was calling them.

Most of all the music warmed little Pasotti's heart. Just yesterday, during a conversation at the Bracco mountain summit, we were talking about this elegant racer, who has great things in mind and who has shown himself to be among the strongest on the climbs. Did the music remind him of certain memorable breaks that have taken place on today's course? And on the short ups and downs of the Capo Mele, Capo Cervo and Capo Berta did he think of emulating some of Coppi's remarkable achievements? All alone he went on the attack—too soon!—right after Alassio where the road started to rear up. He gained some ground. He plummeted down toward Andora like a little falcon, flew up the wide, steep slopes of the Cervo, passing first at Capo Berta as well.

But then there were twenty kilometers of flat roads, and his small lungs, however good they are, did not pump like the forty-plus lungs in concert, climbing behind him and following on his heels. We left him still riding along solo; we hurried to the San Remo finishing line where everyone was waiting for him.

Instead, in the distance, we saw a small group storming in. There were eight of them. And in the final sprint, Pasotti ended up fifth. They had caught up with him, cruelly, just as the vision of victory seemed most to smile on him (and perhaps the friendly sound of the old racer's trumpets was echoing in his mind). Too bad. He battled hard. He had earned it. But men are wolves.

23

THE OLD RACERS' REFRAIN

San Remo, the night of June 8

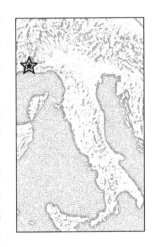

THE BICYCLE HAS TWO WHEELS, ONE THAT guides, the other that runs; one obeys the brain when it comes to deciding whether to go left or right, the other obeys the legs, our professionals' legs: When you touch them, they shout out, "But this is wood!" And for each leg there's a pedal.

The pedals! This is the cross we have to bear. Never, never will they be satisfied: When one is up, its twin is down and each one always wants to do what the other is doing; they continue to run after one another and never, never catch up. Yet who can say no to them? When one is up we push it down, then it's the other one's turn, otherwise an injustice would be done. And the pedals drive the chainwheels, the chainwheels pull the chain, the chain pulls the cog, the cog turns the wheel, and the wheel carries us forward, forward.

The legs! That's the big problem. Some people's are hard and knotty, others' long and tapered like a ballerina's; one has thighs like a hog's, another those of a wading bird, but they are all magnificent, strong, courageous, obedient. Our poor legs! Miserable, enslaved, bruised, hairy, over-sensitive and tired, they carry along, carry along this little piece of machinery coarsely called life.

There are those who study, others, instead, who cultivate the fields, or make clothing or pots, those who manufacture trains or pumps; there are those who care for the sick, or bury the dead; there are those who teach children, and others who say Mass. But we do none of this: We do not manufacture or cultivate anything. We move our legs, see, and nothing else. Absolutely nothing else.

For this reason, we have been given an oddly colored jersey and a number has been put on our back. Then they print our names in the newspaper. They give us money, too, but for how long? They throw flowers at us, love us, kiss us, ask for our autograph. But for how long? Until the day, good people, that our legs say no. They will say: Enough going around and around, pushing pedals up and down. And without a number and a jersey we, too, will sit on our doorstep, on these days in May and June, to watch other legs turning; no longer ours, though. Ours will rest firmly on the ground, like the legs of landowners, like those of pharmacists, teachers, hat makers, plumbers, in sum, like all those who still have all their faculties. And we will say: For us (thank heavens!), no more backbreaking exertion, dust, torment; oh, oh, and no more dysentery. We've had enough of that hellish life of a convict! God, though, how wonderful it was!

Do you remember? The starter, at 8:30 on the dot, lowered his little white flag and off we went together; it was cool; the day was magnificent. They said good-bye to us, but it wasn't a farewell. And very soon, the Venetian, Guido De Santi, broke away, and we pedaled with all our might and main, and the pace was crazy (a gear ratio of 51x15); and we no longer saw the mountains or villas, woods or taverns, nor the laughing, ruddy mouths shouting our poor names; all we saw was the backside of the colleague in front of us, his red jersey bursting with food supplies; and, as we sped along, the loose chippings on the asphalt became long, dizzying streaks. During this time, we relayed each other at the front. And then, who knows how, we found ourselves all alone, remember? For us were reserved the roars and the applause, as well as the banner at the center of town, with a 25,000 lire prize. It was around noon, it was hot, there were no trees to give us a little shade. The good old days, right?

Nineteen hundred forty-nine! Nineteen days of slaving away; at that time, it seemed as though we were falling to pieces.

There will be no more flat tires on that day, no more feeling completely shattered, nor team discipline, nor getting up at the crack of dawn, nor falls into the gutter, nor fines, nor disqualifications, nor the injustices of the esteemed panel of judges, but a comfortable chair on the doorstep in which to sit like a gentleman and watch others sweat blood, at last. All the same, what gratification! Don't you think?

But how? Did you really think we were speaking seriously and we wanted that loathsome chair outside our front

door, so we could die in it little by little? The road is our
agony, but also our daily bread; and at night, when it is
deserted and the moon glistens on the asphalt, the ridiculous dreams of racers like us pass up and down it. And if the
Giro is penal servitude, it is also a great adventure, a game
of kings; it is also war, an outing in the country, an exam,
madness, all those things that greatly remind us of our
youth. And so I ask you: You, the racers, if someone gives
you a purse full of millions, saying to you, "forget it, here is
the money, just give up and stay safely at home, no mud, no
cramps," what would you reply? You reply, "Give up everything, and start rotting in an armchair?" Would you accept,
my wretched friends, old convicts, simple-hearted ones, who
talk about contracts and salaries, yet would sell your souls,
your ugly unfocused souls, for a fine sprint, wouldn't you
wheel ahead of all the others, watched by a huge crowd that
paid to see you? Come on, if you have the courage, answer.
Wouldn't it be a dreadful thing to sell the best of what you
have for scrap paper?

On the mountains, the real mountains, those with ice
on their peaks, those mountains that make us cry and think
of home, it was three o'clock in the afternoon. When we were
just below the crags, the battle signal was given; Coppi
opened fire with a volley of shots along the entire front, and
one by one we fell into the pit of our own perspiration.
Twirling his huge saber, however, Gino Bartali was seen getting up, shakily, to defend his long-standing crown. And people were telling him: You are great!

All around us, girls were there looking at us. They
were shouting, applauding, waving their arms about. Now

we are sorry to tell you this: Sincerely, in everyday life, you are nothing much, but today yes, while you greet us, you are lovely, very beautiful, so many darlings; you seem to be offering yourselves, body and soul. But heaven help you if we were to stop. Then you wouldn't laugh any more, would you? Your faces would harden....

In fact, wherever we go, it is always a holiday: a carnival, playtime, a life of pleasure. There they are! There they are! Who's leading? Hurrah for Gino! Hurrah for everybody! Always Sunday: triumph, prizes, tournament, parade, procession to honor the saint; and everybody is happy, joyful, well fed. And Italy is our velodrome: in the middle of it, we go around and around, with all about us the brave people, 45 million of them, always increasing.

And just as we catch our breath and everyone is chatting together, Mario Vicini took a bad fall and landed on the edge of the road. But it was impossible for us to stop. Then came the lightning, claps of thunder, hail, rain, the shivers began, but we never stopped. When the bottle of tea was empty, when the food was gone, when we had taken the pep pills, not even a cube of sugar was left. Right then came the famous breakaway by numbers 36, 15 and 86. And we asked: Why do we do it?

It's hope that makes us do it (you think that's nothing?): mama waiting at home, sitting by the radio; grandma who is at the hospice; our wife's shoes; cod liver oil for our children.

Keep going, keep going...but for how long? Esteemed race director, with your permission, in due form, we respectfully lodge a complaint. Subject: The distress that, during the race, is unfairly inflicted upon us by mountains too difficult to climb, rebellious legs, hairy, miserable and tired that are on strike this morning and no longer want to drive this little piece of machinery called life. That's why we request a twelve-month extension of time. One more Giro. Is that clear?

The starter will lower his little flag; clean and fresh, we will be on our way, young and old in a single group. With those flashy jerseys we will look like small bouquets of flowers. At least let's make the first steps together, as if we were all the same age. And then what will be, will be....

24

SUPREME JUDGMENT TODAY
ON THE IZOARD

Cuneo, the night of June 9

ICTURE A PROVINCIAL THEATER BURSTING AT the seams with people—Arturo Toscanini conducting! One hour before it is to start there is not a single free seat. Society ladies and gentlemen have made their best efforts to be elegant. People have arrived for the occasion from all over the region. Trepidation, anxiety, palpitations of the heart. As far back as anyone could recall the town had never hosted a similar event. And for the past month people have talked about  nothing else. The entire orchestra is already assembled on the stage. A hum of voices, discordant notes as the instruments softly tune up. Nine o'clock precisely. The lights are dimmed. The audience holds its breath. There he is! A figure in tails and white tie appears from a side door and strides resolutely to the dais. A tremendous burst of applause is unleashed. There he is! Toscanini! But why is his hair black? But it isn't him! It is another. The news flies quickly through the hall. An unfortunate incident has prevented Toscanini from coming. Replacing him is a young maestro whom everybody says is a very capable conductor. The thunderous applause is suspended for a moment, the spectators look at each other, perplexed; then, to show they are up to the standard of good behavior, to avoid humiliating this excellent young man who is not to blame, the hand-clapping resounds once again. But everybody was deeply disappointed.

No different was the state of mind of the crowd that this afternoon in Cuneo poured out along the roads coming into town and on the long home stretch to the finishing line. When the first group of riders made its appearance, a powerful roar welcomed it. But in this roar it was easy to make out the usual two names shouted by thousands of enthusiasts: "Bartali, Coppi!" But Bartali was not there, nor was Coppi. His brother Serse was there among twelve breakaways; the others were decent, experienced young men, and Conte, the winner of the sprint, earned the applause he received. Nevertheless, it wasn't Toscanini.

Why should the columnist be silent about the public's disappointment, which is repeated with depressing regularity since the beginning of the Giro, except for three stages? There was no disappointment at Catania, happy to see its Mario Fazio in first place, nor at Salerno where Coppi won with a sprint, and certainly not in Bolzano where the battle of the Dolomites ended. But in the other thirteen cities, even though they were too tactful to let on, people were very upset. As is well known, feelings are not subject to logic.

And the spirits of the enthusiasts remain impervious to the cold logic that points out the absurdity of their demands. What matters is to be among the leaders in the overall classification; and one can light-heartedly lose all the battles provided victory is achieved in the decisive one. There are two decisive battles: the one in the Dolomites that in fact turned the overall classification upside down and gave big gains to the two "great ones," and tomorrow's conflict in the Alps. But try to convince the fans of this. What long faces they pull seeing their two favorites arrive, without disgrace and without glory, amid the big battalion of latecomers. Their blind love does not waver, but they have a hard time of it and feel they've been betrayed.

During the first stage, while the racers were panting up the steep slopes of the Colle del Contrasto, the "old ones" told us with a superior smile: "These are trifles. You'll see what happens in the Villa San Giovanni-to-Cosenza stage. That one, yes, is definitely an ordeal. At least a third of them will quit. We left Villa San Giovanni, started the murderous ups and downs of the Calabrian mountains, and the very wise ones conceded: "Yes, an exhausting stage, but its importance is relative." That's what they said. "In the Dolomites, ah, in the Dolomites, yes, these boys will sweat blood. Everything is decided up there. It will be a sort of Waterloo."

We went up the whole peninsula, arrived in the Dolomites, climbed the Rolle, and then the Pordoi, then the Passo di Campolongo and the Gardena. The "old ones" looked at us with their little Mephistophelian smile: "Fine stage, it can't be denied. But it takes more than that. A little stroll, this, compared to the French Alps. You'll see, you'll see the Izoard, and then you will let me know!"

Thus, from stage to stage, the wait for the next day's race became a nightmare. Today's stage went by smoothly like an intermezzo—indispensable, yes, because it was necessary to reach the foot of the mountains—but in the end it was superfluous. And in fact if the racers had gone from San Remo to Cuneo by train or motorcoach instead of on their bicycles, the result from the sporting aspect would have been identical. Neither the Colle di San Bartolomeo nor the Colle di Nava were enough to shake the champions; and perfect harmony reigned in their little family as far as the gates of Cuneo, where—just so as not to lose face—came the rebels' usual breakaway.

Tomorrow, then, on the Giro's most difficult stage, the appeal trial in the Bartali case will take place. These days, the enthusiasm for the *campionissimo* after his defeat in the Dolomites has increased enormously, strange as it may seem. The comparison with a trial is justified. The guilty sentence and not the acquittal swells the popularity of the accused. The loser is much more poignant than the winner. And an explosion of enthusiasm never seen before will shake the peninsula tomorrow evening if Bartali were to win back his lost crown. However, it is his last chance. Although he is a man of extraordinary reserves of energy and he does not let adversity dishearten him, it is widely believed that tomorrow he will undergo the last test. Millions of Italians persist, with touching stubbornness, in the belief that he is unbeatable. After the Dolomites they said to themselves: "Of course, Bartali needs to warm up! On the Pordoi he wasn't yet on top form, you will see in the Alps!"

We will see him. An endless flood of good wishes and prayers go with him. But watch out! If he were to yield for the second time tomorrow, it could be an irremediable blow. How fickle is the crowd's love. After so many disappointments, even the most stubborn faith is destroyed. Beware, Bartali! The public is already lining up at the court's entrance. The most famous lawyers have put on their solemn robes, the most compelling arguments are ready, down to the last comma. The judges, that is to say, the mountains, sit enigmatically, their very appearance intimidating. Last appeal: On the course profile, the Dolomites appear like a frightening series of peaks similar to the temperature chart of malarial fever—a total of 3900 meters (12,800 feet) uphill and 3800 meters (12,500 feet) downhill, with four passes to climb over. The profile of tomorrow's mountains is even more impressive and worrisome: Five passes to get over, to wit, the Colle della Maddalena, Col de Vars, Izoard, Montgenèvre and Sestriere—4700 meters (15,400 feet) uphill, 5000 meters (16,400 feet) downhill. It is instinctive to make a comparison with mountaineering: the Civetta wall is terrifying, a classic six grade, but the Eiger, encrusted with green ice, is even more frightening.

On the Col di Nava today, after the racers had gone by, a Bartali fan lost patience with an opposing fan: "But did you see him? Do you want to add ten thousand lire to the bet for tomorrow? You see…you're not ready to bet! But did you see how he was watching Coppi? He covered the last three hundred meters looking behind him, as if he were playing around, and when Coppi took off, what did he do? He wasn't even bothered, I swear. Two, three thrusts of the pedal and he charged ahead again. And he kept on looking behind him…. A cat, absolutely, a cat that amuses himself by killing a mouse! Another twenty thousand lire, look, I bet another twenty thousand lire that tomorrow your Coppi will fall apart!"

25

IN THE ALPS, BARTALI YIELDS TO THE MORE POWERFUL COPPI

Pinerolo, the night of June 10

ODAY, ASCENDING THE IZOARD'S TERRIBLY steep incline, when we saw Bartali set off in solo pursuit with furious thrusts of the pedals, spattered with mud, the corners of his lips turned down in a grimace expressing all of his body's and soul's suffering—Coppi went by quite a while before, and by now he was climbing the final slopes of the pass— there was reborn in us, after thirty years, a feeling that we've never forgotten. Thirty years ago, that is to say, when we learned 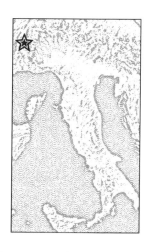 that Hector had been slain by Achilles. Is such a comparison too solemn, too glorious? No. What use would the so-called "classical studies" be if the fragments that remained with us did not become an integral part of our humble existence? Fausto Coppi certainly does not have Achilles's icy cruelty; on the contrary.... Of the two champions he is without a doubt the more cordial and likable. But Bartali, even if he is more aloof and gruff, however unknowingly, lives the same drama as Hector, the drama of a man destroyed by the gods. The Trojan hero finds he is fighting against Athena herself and he was destined to succumb. It's against a superhuman power that Bartali fought, and he could do nothing but lose: the evil power of age. His heart is still formidable; his musculature in perfect condition; and his spirit has kept the firmness of his better days. But time has wreaked havoc on him, without him noticing: little by little it had undermined his marvelous internal organs—nothing much, as neither the doctors nor their instruments registered the slightest change. And yet the man is no longer the same. And today, for the second time, he has lost.

This stage, which devours men—"we've never seen such a dreadfully hard bicycle race," the most experienced technicians were saying this evening—began in a gloomy valley, in the rain, under enormous clouds, in a mist floating just above the ground, in a climate of uneasiness, an atmosphere of depression. Bundled up in their waterproof jackets, the racers, almost as if sheltering from this hostile weather, kept close to one another, dragging themselves up the Valle Stura like big, lethargic snails. Mysteriously, autumn had arrived, the road was deserted—perhaps we would not run into any more towns or human beings, perhaps the caravan would find itself very late this evening, in a wasteland of crags and ice, having used up all its strength, and would never again hear the beloved voices of their dear ones.... That was the frame of mind that reigned. Only sporadically were the misty drapes opened, allowing a glimpse of remote, blackish peaks. But shafts of white light, filtering from under the huge clouds, reminded us that in some part of the earth maybe the sun was shining.

The melancholy troop of fat, ill-treated snails finally emerged from the darkness of the rain above Argentera. We were already quite high up, and the valley was broadening out. We forged ahead and, from the bastions of the Colle della Maddalena, looked down the slippery road whose zigzags disappeared into the bottom of the valley. The sun! And by a stroke of good luck we were able to be present at the decisive scene, at the war's most important engagement, which removed all the doubts, and put an end to the discussions and polemic that gripped the entire country. It was from that very brief scene, taking place in the majestic solitude of the mountains, that all the rest evolved: the triumph of one young man and the inevitable twilight of another, who was no longer young. Hundreds of thousands of Italians would have paid who knows how much to be up there where we were, to see what we were seeing. For years and years— we realized—there would be endless talk about this small occurrence that in itself did not seem to be of special importance: merely a man on a bicycle who was pulling away from his traveling companions. And yet in that instant, and don't laugh, on the side of the road, irresistibly came to pass what the Ancients used to call Destiny.

... then Father Zeus held out his sacred golden scales:
in them he placed two fates of death that lays men low—
one for Achilles, one for Hector breaker of horses
and gripping the beam mid-haft the Father raised it high

*and down went Hector's day of doom, dragging him down
to the strong House of Death …)*[12]

We look down on the racers so steeply that the perspective, almost vertical, transformed them into slender,
colorful insects sliding along extremely slowly. This troop
suddenly quivered lightly here and there. Are they waking up
at last? All of a sudden, one of them, a tiny orange spot,
broke away from the others and very rapidly outdistanced
them. It was Primo Volpi, and we instantly realized from his
colors that he was not one of the giants. However, another of
those little shapes, colored white and blue, immediately
sprang out from the side of the group, arching its back; it
darted ahead and in a few moments had reached the orange
jersey. As the crow flies, at least five hundred meters separated us from them. "But it's Coppi, it's Coppi! You can see
very well it's his style," they shouted. In fact, it really was
him. With impressive speed, if you think of the stiffness of
the incline, he literally flew toward the summit, dragging
with him for three, four switchbacks the little orange spot.
But very soon he was alone.

The drowsy swaying of the group stopped. In Coppi's
wake, two others kicked away sharply, detaching themselves
from the peloton. Then two more. And Bartali? Was our great
one not going to react? Yes! We saw him extricate himself
with difficulty from the middle of the peloton, shift to the
right, and give some sharp heaves on the pedals in their pursuit. But, strangely, it could be said he was doing it without
conviction, that he didn't believe in what he was doing, that

12. Quotes in this chapter are from "The Iliad" by Homer.

he assumed all that commotion was a fairly harmless ruse. We then got back in the car, and amid thick, ill-mannered clouds and alternating shafts of sunlight, we reached the Passo della Maddalena, losing sight of the racers,

We would see only two more of them the rest of the way to Pinerolo. The fugitive and the one pursuing him, the two greatest heroes, fighting tooth and nail for the kingdom. The others remained behind, farther and farther behind, separated by high valleys and precipices, battling strenuously among themselves; but from this moment on, they were out of the running. Everything came down to that, to this battle between the two solo riders, and hearts were gripped with emotion. When we had descended the tricky Maddalena road at breakneck speed to a dark valley, we met the French gendarmes stationed at every intersection, as if welcoming us, we heard the echo of voices different from ours; the road, really steep and still encircled by crags, rose up mercilessly toward the Col de Vars; other mountains appeared, all gloomy and wild (behind us, for only a few moments, appeared an immense turreted rock with impressive, gigantic purplish pilasters of ice). We began to understand why people said the Dolomites' stage was a joke compared to today's. The Colle della Maddalena would already have sufficed to break the back of an ox. And we had barely begun.

Victory took its place at Coppi's side right from the first moments of the duel. Anyone who saw him no longer had any doubts. His pace up those cursed climbs had irresistible power. Who could have stopped him? Every so often, to relieve the discomfort of the saddle he raised himself up on the pedals; and so light was he, he looked as though he wanted to stretch just to rid himself of excess energy, as an athlete does on awakening from a deep sleep. The muscles under the skin were visible, resembling extraordinarily young snakes about to come out of their sheaths. As in the Dolomites, he moved forward in absolute calm, almost as if he were unaware that a wolf followed right on his heels. From his team car, which stayed always at his side, Zambrini watched him, smiling, now certain of the victory.

"Athena rushed to Achilles, her bright eyes gleaming,
standing shoulder-to-shoulder, winging orders now:
"At last our hopes run high, my brilliant Achilles—
Father Zeus must love you—
we'll sweep great glory back to Achaea's fleet,
we'll kill this Hector, mad as he is for battle!"

On the border, near the Colle della Maddalena, he had more than two minutes advance; and on the Colle de Vars summit, four minutes twenty-nine seconds. Now, at the bottom of a long, frightful gorge, the disturbing wall of the Izoard appears. So for Bartali, was this the final collapse? The bad weather, which once was his faithful ally, had not given him any help? Has his legendary resistance suddenly failed him? No, Bartali was always himself: stubborn, tough, relentless. But how does one resist someone favored by the gods? He was filthy with mud, but his face, grey with dirt, remained unmoved by the exertion. He kept on pedaling as if some hideous beast were running after him and he knew that if he were caught all hope was lost. It was only time, irreparable time, that was running after him. And it was an inspiring sight to see this man, alone in the wild gorge, engaged in a desperate battle with his years.

"And now death, grim death is looming up beside me,
no longer far away. No way to escape it now. This,
this was their pleasure after all, sealed long ago—
Zeus and the son of Zeus, the distant deadly Archer—
though often before now they rushed to my defense.
So now I meet my doom. Well, let me die—
but not without struggle, not without glory, no,
in some great clash of arms that even men to come
will hear down all the years!"

Without being able to see one another because every minute the barrier of gorges, crags, forests widened between them, the adversaries fought to the very end. Here come the fantastic terraces of the Izoard, which would even take an eagle's breath away, and that end in a bleak amphitheater of huge, abrupt crags, with towers of yellow rock that appear human. Then comes the dizzying climb above Briançon, a vertical elevation of a thousand meters (3280 feet). And that's not enough. There is still the Montgenèvre ascent, an additional five hundred meters of climbing. Was that the moment when this massacre finished? No, it wasn't finished. There is a fifth wall to scale, the Sestriere, the ultimate torture, destined to chastise these men for their sins: another half-kilometer of mountain climbing to grind out on the pedals. What do the details of a report matter in so great a battle? How much weight can be attributed in the final reckoning to Coppi's five flat tires and Bartali's three? Coppi flies on toward the summit, no longer worried by the apprehension he had during the first hours, certain now to reach the finishing line alone. And Bartali holds out. But little by little the minutes between them accumulate. 6:46 at Montgenèvre, 7:17 at Cesana, almost 8:00 at Sestriere; and nearly a dozen minutes at the Pinerolo stadium.

A loser, today, Bartali, for the first time. That's what fills us with bitterness, because it reminds us intensely of our common fate. Today, for the first time, Bartali understood that he has reached his twilight years. And for the first time he smiled. With our own eyes, as we passed close to him, we observed the phenomenon. A person at the side of the road waved to him. And he, turning his head slightly in that direction, smiled; that cantankerous, off-putting, disagreeable man, the unmanageable bear with the eternal sullen grimace of unhappiness, him? Yes him, he actually smiled. Why did you do it, Bartali? Don't you know that by doing so you have destroyed the prickly spell that protected you? Are you beginning to appreciate the applause, the hurrahs of people who don't know you? So, is it the weight of your years? You have accepted it, at last.

26

COMPETING AGAINST THEMSELVES
FROM PINEROLO TO TURIN

Turin, the night of June 11

THE TIME TRIAL STAGE: THE ONLY COMPETITION in which the last arrive first, and the first arrive last. Riders depart from Pinerolo every four minutes, beginning with those whose abilities are the most modest. The pink jersey will be the last to leave.

It is a race in which you have to be calculating: the racer cannot challenge anyone but himself, the friendly wheel is no longer there to pull you, nor the incitement of your adversary to spur you on; also gone are the tactical maneuvers among teammates. At last the *gregari* can play at being stars; there is no danger that the team leader will ask for a wheel or send them to buy cold orangeade. The spectator has no way of knowing who is winning or losing—like today, when everyone was paying attention to the aces and after having computed the odds concluded Coppi would win, forgetting about Bevilacqua who, having purposely husbanded his energy yesterday in the Alps, took off like an express train at an average speed of forty-two kilometers an hour, that is, faster than all the other starters; and they paid no attention to Corrieri or De Santi, who were also faster than the *campionissimo*; it seemed that he didn't commit himself too much.

The excitement generated by a race of this kind is somewhat theoretical: It is measured at the little tables where all the calculations are completed and the numbers are compared. The racers' rival is the hand of the stopwatch that is released at the start and stopped at the finish. How far has it run in between?

To see them as they start off alone, faces tense and flushed, it is hard to understand why the champions are so uneasy. It could be said that so much effort is expended in vain. And a feeling of dreariness permeates the event, as it does in all solitary endeavors: What comes to mind is the chess player who frets over a problem; without an adversary, the lonely retiree concentrating on a game of solitaire; the self-taught who has no free days and in the evening studies English through a correspondence school or from phonograph records. In short, after seventeen days of body-to-body combat, it resembles a phlegmatic target-shooting competition.

The last starts first: His name is Carollo, a day-laborer by trade, who deprived Malabrocca of last place in the overall classification, below which there is no one. It's a placing that many would like: the last one arouses the public's curiosity and sympathy quite a lot more than does the seventh or eighth in the classification. The last one becomes, in a sense, the standard bearer of all the destitute and the needy on this earth; he's considered a sort of brother by all those who, in the arena of life, have failed to find even standing room in the Grand Lodge—and perhaps not even that. But in addition to the sentimental interest in the placing, a concrete advantage has been tacked on this year. Every day bundles of money orders and checks from all over Italy are delivered to the Giringiro whose idea it was to give a prize to the racer who achieves this inverted glory. Factory workers, schoolchildren, priests, teachers, provincial landowners have contributed to this perquisite for the so-called "black jersey." And it has been estimated that Carollo, by dint of losing, will pick up more than two hundred thousand lire.

What a strange feeling it must be for him to be first: in front of him, two traffic policemen on motorcycles, clearing the road; behind, a car just for him, with his name on the grill and the back; and at the edges of the fields people applauding—not many, to be truthful, because the army of sports enthusiasts will show up later in alarming numbers to pay tribute to the greatest champions. For the public, one must admit, no stage is more enjoyable than this one. The entertainment is not limited to two or three seconds—the time that it takes a peloton of cyclists to pass by in front of them—but it goes on for hours; and it doesn't cost anything. Finally! There is no longer the anxiety of having to single out Bartali's or Coppi's number from the seething tangle of caps and jerseys. On the contrary, all the aces can be savored one by one without any fear of confusing them; and you also have time to talk things over before the next one arrives.

So he goes, the blond Carollo, absolutely unconcerned about the behavior of his closest rival, Malabrocca, next to last in the classification, who left four minutes after him. A gap of more than two hours separates them and it's hard to contemplate Malabrocca going so slowly over a sixty-five kilometer route that he can pull a fast one and pinch his title. Not even if he were to walk from time to time. Now and then, Carollo can even entertain dreams of victory. Who knows, those huge clouds on the mountain may unleash a storm and surprise the competitors starting after him.... Who knows, the wind may blow hard enough to knock them out of the saddle, immobilizing them in the middle of the road until nightfall.... And he, making a powerful leap forward, tomorrow will put on the pink jersey.... But these are just jokes. The clouds have burst, emptying their waters all along the road, but it was just an ordinary, harmless June rainfall. In reality, everything has now been decided; if anything can change in the classification, it certainly doesn't involve the first place. The Giro—at least this is the professors' opinion—has nothing of further importance to reveal, not even in tomorrow's stage that will take us to Monza. And spirits are already a bit enervated by sadness, as is always the case when the end is near; it doesn't matter whether the ending is beautiful or ugly, because man then realizes how fast time flies and how short life is.

In any case, the battle today concerns second place, because Leoni was only three-and-a-half minutes behind Bartali, and time trials have never been Bartali's forte. But it did not go well for Leoni today, partly because he has a large boil; he let himself be passed by Coppi after no more than twenty kilometers, so instead of a step up in the classification, he slipped down and left third place to Cottur.

And Bartali? Today, too, Bartali demonstrated his great honesty as a racer, doing his utmost as if he were going for the win. And he well knew that, today, victory would not be his. At Pinerolo, waiting for the starter to call him and trying to free himself from a mob of boys besieging him with postcards and pencils, wanting an autograph, the loser on the Izoard took refuge in our car. He was serene, seemed in perfect form, and was unusually talkative. He started to complain—he had to grumble about something in order to remain the real Bartali—because Leoni was scheduled to leave after him instead of vice versa. So, he said, that he did not have the chance to regulate his speed with regard to Leoni's pace, but Leoni could do so with regard to his. Then he asked us: "And you, who will you follow in your car? Coppi, right?" For a moment there was a note of bitterness in his voice. "Oh, everybody will follow Coppi today. He's riding well. I don't know how to any more!" He said it, though, without rancor, as if it seemed logical to him and he had resigned himself to it.

Then he spoke about yesterday's stage. He said that when Coppi took off, he thought it was a prank. But he did not offer any justification, quite the contrary. He did not rebel. And he spoke as if he were just talking to himself, to convince himself. "You see, I am no longer the same…. Now I am afraid in the descents…. Yesterday, down the Izoard, I lost two minutes…. In the past. I shot off into space. Now I am afraid. When I see a sharp turn I slow down…. Who knows, perhaps it is also the Torino accident. That shocked me. In the past I flew downhill, I went hard…. Now I race hard uphill, but not downhill any more. I am afraid now!"

Then a voice from the starting line was heard calling him. Bartali adjusted his pigskin mitts, got out of the car, and went toward his bicycle just like a man on his way to work.

27

COPPI HAS WON THE GIRO D'ITALIA

Milan, June 13
[by Ciro Verratti]

IDEAS ABOUT ITALIAN CYCLING HAVE BEEN clarified. And if, at the end of this Giro d'Italia, there are still people who do not see the light, it means they are nearsighted and need thick glasses. It's Fausto Coppi who won, as we had foreseen, and as the logic of cycling dictated, a logic that in truth was not embraced by many critics who up to the eve of the decisive stage were still perplexed and tormented by doubts. But it is not our intention to start an argument here; we wish only to make an observation that in point of fact gives us no pleasure. Coppi's victory, particularly the style with which he achieved it, puts a new face on Italian cycling and takes the spice out of an incentive that, until now, made our sport so popular. Until yesterday it was still possible to talk about a Coppi-Bartali rivalry, a rivalry that excited the crowds and gave them shudders of passionate ardour. We must confess today that this rivalry is only a memory because Bartali, a champion of undoubted valor, cannot stand up to a comparison with Coppi.

The final stronghold of Bartali's supporters was the French Alps; it was that hellish race taking place on impossible roads fit only for the chamois, dug out of the barren ground—in short, the race that requires not only exceptional class but a quasi-heroic tolerance of pain. It was said that Coppi had the class, but was unable to suffer like Bartali. Bartali, in contrast, was indeed the man to cope with the "extremely difficult," the man who best knew how to shine the more brutal the effort. Well, Coppi captured the last line of defense held by Bartali's partisans! He showed that in Bartali's kingdom he was indeed the king.

On the Izoard's frighteningly sinuous roads, where half the Giro's cars were forced to stop, Coppi said there was no obstacle that could deter him, that he likes anything that is difficult and out of reach, and finds it stimulating and exciting. Coppi, therefore, dominated Bartali on those roads where Bartali had dominated all the others, Italians as well as foreigners.

There are bad days in cycling, and a bad day for Bartali could have given rise to questions still hanging. We wouldn't have been at all surprised because Coppi has bad days, too; in fact he is very familiar with them. However, there is nothing of this kind. On the contrary, in the French mountains, Bartali rode a great race, he showed his mettle as a champion, but unfortunately he found his master in Coppi. So we feel it's hazardous to speak of revenge or hopes of reversing the positions because Gino, a champion that we have trouble imagining to be on the decline, couldn't have done better. It's Coppi who did better than him. There is nothing left to do but accept the fact and assign to Coppi the position he is entitled to: *numero uno* in Italian cycling, or rather, in world cycling. Today there is a gap between him and Bartali, but also a gap between Bartali and all the others. One is first, the other is second; and both are the pride of Italy's sports world. Everybody envies us our two champions, starting with the French. We only hope that Bartali will hang in there: he is the necessary element of comparison for determining Coppi's class.

After the Monza sprint, more than one person asked us this question: "Coppi, when he wants to, dominates the others. Why does he want to so rarely?" Herein lies a little of the mystery surrounding this champion's delicate psychological make-up. The truth is that Coppi does not need the glory of a single day; he does not race for immediate applause, he looks farther ahead. He has plans of his own to realize, a strategy that requires giving up certain things. This kind of self-interest perhaps does not find favor with those who generously applaud him along the roads or climb to the top of the mountains for the thrill of the moment, but it's a hard fact—you have to ration your efforts with much vigilance; it's what the experts call "wisdom." Naturally, the delirious crowds of sports enthusiasts prefer romantic adventure over bourgeois yawns, but not every day in life can be an occasion for adventure or romance. There are also days of peace, moments of mediocrity, hours of dullness bereft of emotion. One can like Coppi a lot or not at all, one can even hold against him the wise administration of his strength, but one must admit he is the strongest. If you want, go right ahead and scold him for not always wanting to work hard, but you must admit that when he does feel like it, he creates a masterpiece. The last one he created goes by the name of the Izoard.

Now we must say something about Leoni who, up until the famous Alps stage, was the Giro's pink jersey and could have won if Coppi and Bartali, as had sometimes happened in other circumstances, had paralyzed each other. When the battle of the Alps flared up, Leoni was unable to defend himself with the same courage he had shown in the Dolomites. This time the mountain was relentless, too hostile to him, the acknowledged friend of the plains and sprints. However, no one would have snatched his well-deserved third place, if fate had not been so unfair to him the day of the time trial. That day he was not beaten by his adversaries, he was beaten by a boil. It is not a very noble injury, but one all the same. He managed to repress his tears of pain and continue to pedal, as if there were no problem, but he lost more and more ground and had to resign himself to bitter defeat. He deserves our praises, as does Cottur, a brave, tenacious racer who is the same age as Bartali and shares his burning passion. Along with him we must praise all his colleagues on the Wilier Triestina team who, even without Magni, managed to earn a flattering placing in the team race. Astrua conquered, and defended vigorously and courageously his white jersey, and in certain moments he was as worthy as the strongest. We would like to mention other deserving racers, but we are obliged to come back to that later, due to the lack of space.

Now we must tell you about the final stage, which was more than anything else a triumphal march toward the ultimate finishing line. It was a stage in which, more than to the individual racers, the triumph belonged to the Giro with all the crowds and all its enthusiasm it unleashes. On certain roads in Lombardy, the crowd did not leave even a narrow corridor open and occasionally we had to use the car as a wedge to open up a passage. And yet those people waited for hours and we were late; and they still smiled as they looked at us, but with obvious impatience. They were waiting for Coppi and Bartali, naturally, but most of all they were awaiting the Giro, for all the splendor and symbolism it embodied.

We left early from Turin and headed toward Vercelli and Novara at the pace of a procession. There was also a strong wind, however, and that slowed us down. Along the roads of Piedmont, the enthusiasm was lukewarm; and perhaps for this reason we felt the welcome in Lombardy particularly affectionate. At Novara, Conte and Bevilacqua were the protagonists at the intermediate sprint, won by Conte; but we have to say that Bevilacqua was hindered by a policeman who stupidly got in front of him just as he took off for the final sprint. We drove along tens of kilometers of roads black with spectators, and then followed the shore of Lake Como that had never looked as enchanting as it did yesterday, under that bright afternoon sun.

And so we arrived at the foot of the Ghisallo, the mountain famous for its dust and the battles that have taken place there. We already knew that Coppi was not going to commit himself, as we had known the day before that he would not push himself hard during the time trial. However, on those slopes that had so often been witnesses to the superior class of the champion in the white-and-blue jersey, we hoped for a possible battle inspired by the circumstances, if not by design. Instead, nothing remarkable happened and Bartali, who remained vigilant, managed to be first across the King of the Mountains sprint line, thanks to some powerful pedal thrusts; he was followed by Pasotti, Martini, Vittorio Magni and Coppi, in that order. The crowd was no less delirious because the sacred fire of Bartali admirers has not died out, but smolders under the ashes of defeat. Give Bartali's fans a hint of victory and from those ashes flames will be unleashed.

Then, on the descent, the riders came back together, and as far as Milan it was a controlled race in a happy, festive atmosphere. It was the Giro d'Italia presented to us in its most glowing colors. On the Monza track the final sprint favored Corrieri, who won ahead of Ricci and Fausto Coppi, after an interminable lap around the autodrome. It made an odd impression on us to hear the soft rustling of wheels on that asphalt that had until now known only the ear-splitting voices of engines.

The Giro seemed endless, and yet it is over. We must be grateful to Emilio De Martino, director of *La Gazzetta dello Sport*, for the daring inventiveness that characterized the Giro and for guiding it safely to port. It all looked to be exceptionally difficult: the departure from Sicily, the mighty mountain stages and the intermediate sprints. The road seemed strewn with stumbling blocks, but it became obvious that enthusiasm and tenacity can overcome even the greatest obstacles. Some rough spots were encountered just where they were least expected, in time-tested areas. It is necessary that the central organization more attentively oversees the local stage organizations. Several deficiencies were noted, for example, at the Naples and Genoa finishes. These are small flaws, however, that do not mar the harmony of a beautiful race.

It was a difficult Giro d'Italia: It gave us some days of boredom; other days, it is undeniable, of profound dejection; but there were also moments of unforgettable emotion; and even we, who are quite hardened by professional routine, experienced hours of elation, almost as great as that of the fans on the Pordoi, Abetone and Ghisallo. Many times we cried out for it to end, but now that it has ended, we're sorry that it's over; now that it's gone, we miss it.

How many kilometers in tomorrow's stage? There is no stage tomorrow. A real shame!

28

THE SUPERNATURAL,
IN ITS CYCLING FORM,
WILL NEVER REACH THE END

Milan, June 13

N THE MIDDLE OF THE IMMENSE TIDE OF CARS that ebbed slowly from the Monza autodrome the day before yesterday—backlit by the setting sun's fading rays, it looked like a herd wreathed in dust that one sees in westerns—here and there, lost in this gigantic chaos, some spots of vivid color stood out. It was the racers, still wearing their jerseys and transfigured by the exertion; some were perched on the team cars among the spare wheels, others leaned out of a truck's rear window, and others were still on their bicycle saddles because no one, in this throng, had bothered to give them a lift; and so they had fifteen kilometers of extra effort to complete the Giro—adding to four-thousand kilometers already done.

They saw us: they saw our dusty car, our official nameplate, our sun-baked faces. We belonged to the same gang: them and us, fragments of a small, fascinating world that was at last dispersing to re-enter the dullness of everyday life. We looked at each other with a sad, understanding smile; like soldiers returning from war who, in the hubbub of a big railway station, are immediately considered as brothers. During the Giro, we and the racers had remained virtual strangers; but now, no, now all the others were strangers and we instead were suddenly friends, we alone in that crowd could understand each other, parties to a secret full of melancholy.

For nineteen days, we had seen them gallop throughout the entire peninsula with great astonishment, their legs the sole source of energy, and we then watched them continue in the Alps, on the climbs and descents, right next to precipices. One hundredth of what the last of them had done would have crushed us even twenty years ago when we were young, and we would have been taken to the hospital for at least a month. What remained now of all this frightful labor? Had it produced anything? Nothing. Pure fatigue, then, offered in sacrifice to a senseless mania?

And yet, as soon as these men proceeded, passing from city to city, the people—astonishingly!—abandoned their business or their spade, jumped out of bed, came down from the remotest homesteads, traveled very long distances on foot, waited in the rain and sun for entire mornings, and, there they were, the people of all Italy, farmers, laborers, old salts, mothers, decadent old men, paralytics, priests, beggars, thieves, massed along four thousand kilometers, and they weren't what they were the day before, a new, powerful feeling possessed them, they were laughing, yelling, the sorrows of life forgotten for a few instants, they were happy, without a doubt, and we can vouch for that here.

Does something as crazy and preposterous as the Giro d'Italia by bicycle serve a purpose, then? Of course it does: it's one of the last meccas of the imagination, a stronghold of romanticism, besieged by the gloomy forces of progress, and it refuses to surrender.

Look at them, as they pedal and pedal through the fields, hills and forests. They are pilgrims traveling to a distant city that they will never reach: they symbolize, in flesh and blood, as depicted in an ancient painting, the incomprehensible adventure of life. That's what it is—pure romanticism.

They are knights errant who leave for a war where there are no lands to be conquered: and the giants who are their enemies resemble the windmills of Don Quixote, they have neither human limbs nor faces, they are called distance, grade, suffering, rain, fear, tears and wounds. And this, too, is rather romantic.

They are young slaves, prisoners of an ogre who has tied them to an enormous leaden grinder and they churn around, flogged till the blood runs, and from the surrounding woods their women call, weeping, but the slaves cannot reply. And is this not romanticism?

They are madmen, because they could cover the same ground without exerting themselves, and instead they labor like animals; they could go slowly, and instead they wear themselves out to speed along flat out; almost all of them could earn the same amount of money without suffering, and instead they prefer the agony. Yes, here, too, is some romanticism.

And they are also monks; belonging to a special brotherhood ruled by its own, tough laws. Each one of them hopes for grace, but it is granted to very few, one or two per decade.

Yet they continue because they know that the world will confer on the chosen few, without even being aware of it, a sort of sacred investiture. And then the glory will be dazzling. A pure fairytale, this, too, worthy of times long past.

But now the fairytale has come to an end. The knights errant, the pilgrims, the madmen, the monks have gone back home: these are ordinary men, surrounded by their mothers, wives and toddlers; free, and a little sad. The finish banner where prizes were contested has been most carefully taken and placed in the storage room of the Association "Velo e Sport" of Saveria Mannelli. The graze on Mario Fazio's right elbow is already healing. The complaint made by racer Croci-Torti concerning the three thousand-lire fine (for repeated holding onto one of the official cars) begins its eternal slumber among the international jury's notebooks piled in a closet at *La Gazzetta dello Sport*. The aluminum flask that Gino Bartali contemptuously flung away three kilometers after Cervieres has by chance been found by a young shepherd and now dangles from his belt. In a gutter between Cagli and Acqualunga, where it had crawled to die, the ants have already devoured almost half of the stray dog run over by one of the caravan's radio trucks. And the sun, the wind, the rain nibble away at the cardboard posters nailed to the larches below the Passo di Pordoi, and which urge the fans: "Do not push the racers!" It looked as if there would be no end to it, and it is already a part of the past. Today people are talking about other things, of the Giro del Lazio, of the Tour de France (is it or isn't it true that Bartali doesn't want to race on the same team as Coppi?), of velodromes, of the Tour of Switzerland, of what tomorrow will bring. Such is life!

And next year, in May, the starter will once more lower his flag, and again the year after that, and so on, spring after spring, the enchantment will live on. Until the day (but will we still be alive?) when reasonable people will say it is absurd to continue; by then, bicycles will have become rare, almost comical scrap metal, used by a few nostalgic maniacs, and voices will be raised ridiculing the Giro d'Italia.

No, don't give up, bicycle. By then we will probably be dead and buried. Coppi will be an emaciated, shaking little grandfather unknown to the new generations; other names will be shouted by the crowds. Do not yield, oh "divine bicycle," as Henri Desgrange, the Tour's patron has said. If you were to surrender it would mean the end, not only of an era in sports, a chapter in civilization; but also put an even greater restriction on what is left of the realm of illusion, where simple souls find relief. At the risk of seeming ridiculous, take off again on a cool May morning, and travel the ancient roads of Italy. By then we will be traveling mostly by rocket trains; atomic energy will be sparing us the least little effort; we will be extremely powerful and civilized. Pay no attention to us, bicycle. Just fly along, with your frail strength, by mountains and valleys, sweat, strive and suffer. From his isolated alpine hut, the woodcutter will still come down to shout hurrah, fishermen will climb up from the beach, accountants will abandon their ledgers, the blacksmith will let the fire die so he can come to celebrate you, the poets, the dreamers, the good, and the humble people, still sensitive to kindness, will still crowd the edges of the roads, forgetting poverty and hardship, thanks to you. And the young girls will cover you with flowers.

AFTERWORD

I HAVE NEVER FORGOTTEN WHAT I HAD READ BACK IN 1949 AS A
boy who "rooted" for Bartali—though still admiring Fausto
Coppi: I was a voracious reader, especially of newspaper
articles. When the *Corriere della Sera* sent Dino Buzzati to
follow the Giro, I was happily surprised, and the first few
articles were enough to make me aware that something worthy of Buzzati was taking shape, and that, as in all the
reports of this author, his imagination was getting the better
of the reporting, swallowing it and making it his.

Buzzati was best known for his novels and short stories: "Bàrnabo of the Mountains," 1933; "The Secret of the
Old Forest," 1935; "The Tartar Steppe," 1940; "The Seven
Messengers," 1942; and his many articles published in the
Corriere della Sera—first as a war correspondent, then as a
special correspondent, and as the writer of literary articles
published on the cultural page. At the Giro, it was immediately clear that Buzzati was composing a tale that, besides
being typically his, was one that was forming a single
homogenous narrative; and that the Giro offered him a
design of rare adaptability to his style of writing. On the
backdrop of the Giro, the faces in the anonymous crowd

were those of the common people of an Italy in which all of us, the war having just ended, were rediscovering the hope of a better tomorrow. The Giro was building its myth, reborn every day, after every evening's dissolution. In the foreground rose the story of a man threatened by age, Bartali, "the old man"—at one point called Hector, as if he were a hero from Homer—confronted by the stature and brilliance of the younger Fausto Coppi—Achilles—who was destined to strike the death blow and, guided by the hand of Fate, had to choose "that precise moment."

"Bartali, the old lion" Buzzati writes from Naples, when after the Pratola climb, fifty kilometers from Salerno, where Coppi tries a sudden acceleration and for a few minutes "the old man" had a hard time following him—"is this the day that sooner or later had to come, is this your supreme hour after which the last collapse of youth begins? [...] Suddenly, you know, the mysterious talent will have to leave you. In the middle of a race, all at once, you will feel strangely alone: like a king at the height of battle, who, on turning to issue orders, no longer sees his army, dissolved by magic into nothingness. This terrible moment will come. But when? You don't know. And it could be this very day...."

This is the Buzzati who created Drogo, the "Tartar Steppe" narrator who shatters the limits of reality on the extreme limits of space and time, and who awaits the fatal blow, or for glory (it doesn't matter) from this enemy hidden beyond the horizon. From the very first articles, Buzzati sets the tone of the report with a military metaphor he adheres to faithfully: The cyclists, like a group of little soldiers, advance toward an enemy consisting of rain, wind, ascents and endless kilometers; behind them, general staffs, officers and subalterns operating mysteriously, devising strategies, tactical plans, traps, etc.... What they are condemned to will emerge from the war: the real enemy, against which cunning cannot be used—the high mountains, the Alps and the Dolomites, rising like a Kafkian Court of Justice. "The judges, that is, the mountains, preside, enigmatic...."

This is the Buzzati we know best: the novel "A Love Affair," 1963, marks a turning point in the writer's narrative course, and the themes and the writing will change (though the poet who created Drogo does not disappear entirely), will enter the era of painting, comic strips, art criticism. But for us the Buzzati that counts (perhaps there is a Buzzati for every generation: perhaps each generation has had and will have its own desert) is here, in this critical expectation: perfectly placed in the years of fascism's decline and those of the cold war, when the enemy was tangible, the threat constant, the waiting a daily, agonizing presence.

This discussion could take us far (and would also point out Buzzati's political-civil roots that the critics hardly take into consideration). As for Bartali-Hector, the moment came on the Izoard. At that point, however, character and situation had already merged completely on the edge of the abyss, and the character, as always in this Buzzati, was absorbed by the situation, had become an element of a higher operation. Like "the desert," the Giro becomes a spatial dimension, and time, in a vertical sense, digs into things. It is only a matter of waiting. After all, even the Giro will end up in the nothingness of things that happened because, Buzzati says, everything soon comes to an end and "man realizes how time flies and how brief life is."

Of course, there are other things in the myth of the Giro: for post-war Italians the atmosphere of fervent moral renewal, the discovery of the landscape and the region (see the crossing of the Apennines from Rome to Pesaro in Chapter 12), the memory of the ruins and the losses (the stupendous Chapter 11 on Cassino, with its dead rising from the earth), a restrained patriotism where Trieste is concerned.... Let us not forget that Buzzati the journalist (as few others) had a keen sense of smell for a fact, for the story; that in newspaper stories he continually found food for his narratives; and that, when all is said and done, journalism and narrative reporting and storytelling fact and fantasy merged so closely in him as to justify the recurring suspicion that an occult favoritism worked miraculously for him.

Bartoli-Hector has every right to stand with Bàrnabo, Drogo, the "messengers" and the other characters, already created or about to be given birth. The profession offered him a golden opportunity, and the writer seized it with the spontaneity and hard-working candor (the profession equates with duty as well) of children who live in harmony with the world of their games. Written at the end of each stage and thus within a time limit, then dictated to the newspaper, the articles are perfect and perfectly tied to one another. A notebook, unfortunately incomplete, lovingly kept by his wife Almerina, shows from the very first entries jotted down in unsteady handwriting and a few sketches, as he rode in a car (Buzzati traveled with Ciro Verratti, sports reporter for the *Corrieree d'informazione*) how imagination devoured reality and the romance or the myth replaced it by simply using the plain facts. "Cuneo—rain—racers in weatherproof jackets—we enter a dark valley—Valle Stura (see the sketch of the valley with three snails going up)—clearing— more rain—increasing gloom—autumn has come—nobody— uncomfortable humidity—everybody quit?—Pietraporzio— clearing—Argentera—stops raining—sun—town visible— one breaks away (red)—another keeps close behind—then Coppi breaks away then Volpi—then two others, then Bartali [...]—deformed pine trees—we begin to climb again in a dark gorge...."

The facts in the report become spare and allusive, yet remain scrupulously precise. Buzzati not only skips over it, but gives the impression he already knows it. The fall of Bartali-Hector, in effect, is not only expected but accepted, just as the decline of all things battling against time are expected and accepted. It is as if everything were already prepared and remained only to be transcribed. Rarely, as in this case, does Buzzati write as if his words are meant to voice something previously written, to mirror a thing set forth in a page that exists elsewhere, in which reality reflects the distinctive features of futility.

— Claudio Marabini

Claudio Marabini is an Italian scholar and writer who had the idea to create this book in 1980.

STAGE RESULTS
AND GENERAL CLASSIFICATION
FROM THE 32ND GIRO D'ITALIA, 1949

Stage 1, Palermo-Catania

1. Mario Fazio, 261km in 7:47:55 (average 33.467 kph, time bonus 2:00); 2. Carrea, at six bicycle-lengths (time bonus 0:45); 3. Cottur, at 1:17 (time bonus 0:15); 4. Fausto Coppi, at 2:21; 5. Corrieri; 6. Bartali; 7. Leoni; 8. Schaer; 9. Luciano Maggini; 10. Logli; followed by a group of 13 racers, all with the same time as Coppi.

Mountains Grand Prix

Contrasto: 1. M. Fazio, 6pts; 2. Monari, 4pts; 3. Carrea, 3pts.

Stage 2, Catania-Messina

1. Sergio Maggini, 163km in 4:46:46 (average 33.985 kph, bonus 1:00); 2. Cottur, at 0:30 (bonus 0:30); 3. Schaer, at 0:45 (bonus 0:15); 4. Ronconi; 5. De Santi, both s.t.; 6. Jomaux, at 1:13; 7. Pezzi; 8. Frosini, both s.t.; 9. Corrieri, at 2:24; 10. Servadei; a big group of racers, including the Coppi brothers, Bartali, etc., all with the same time as Corrieri.

Overall after Stage 2: 1. Cottur, 12:36:13; 2. Carrea, at 1:07; 3. M. Fazio, at 1:18; 4. Schaer, at 1:34; ; 5. Ronconi, at 1:49; 6. Jomaux and Pezzi, at 3:02; 8. Martini, at 3:43; 9. Corrieri, F. Coppi, Logli, Bartali, Leoni, Astrua, Brignole, Bresci, Croci-Torti, Drei, Simonini, Volpi, L. Maggini, tied at 4:13.

Stage 3, Villa San Giovanni-Cosenza

1. De Santi, 214km in 7:02:31 (average 30.817 kph, bonus 1:00); 2. Pasotti, at 2:08 (bonus 0:30); 3. L. Maggini, at 2:58 (bonus 0:15); 4. Soldani; 5. Leoni; 6. Martini; 7. M. Fazio, all s.t.; 8. Jomaux, at 3:13 (bonus 1:00); 9. Ronconi; 10. Peverelli; then came a group of 51 racers including Bartali, F. Coppi, Cottur, Carrea, all with the same time as Maggini.

Mountains Grand Prix

Tiriolo: 1. Jomaux, 6pts; 2. Logli, 4pts; 3. F. Coppi, 3pts.

Overall after Stage 3: 1. Cottur, 19:42:57; 2. Carrea, at 1:07; 3. M. Fazio, at 1:18; 4. Schaer, at 1:34; 5. Ronconi, at 1:49; 6. Jomaux, at 2:02; 7. Pezzi, at 3:02; 8. Martini and Logli, at 3:43; 10. F. Coppi and L. Maggini, at 3:58; 12. Bartali, at 4:13.

Stage 4, Cosenza-Salerno
1. F. Coppi, 292km in 9:59:21 (average 29.300 kph, bonus 1:00); 2. Leoni (bonus 0:30); 3. Bartali (bonus 0:15); 4. Soldani; 5. Drei; 6. Frosini; 7. Barozzi; 8. Logli; 9. Ricci; 10. M. Fazio, and a group of racers all with the same time as Coppi.

Overall after Stage 4: 1. Cottur, 29:42:18; 2. M. Fazio, at 1:18; 3. Schaer and Ronconi, at 1:34; 5. Jomaux, at 2:02; 6. Carrea, at 2:55; 7. F. Coppi, at 2:58; 8. Pezzi, at 3:02; 9. De Santi, at 3:33; 10. Logli, Martini and Leoni, at 3:43; 13. Bartali, at 3:58.

Stage 5, Salerno-Naples
1. Biagioni, 161km in 4:36:24 (average 34.943 kph, bonus 1:00); 2. Leoni, at 4:02 (bonus 0:30); 3. L. Maggini (bonus 0:15); 4. F. Coppi; 5. Logli; 6. Soldani; 7. Bartali; 8. Pasotti: tied for ninth place, 26 other racers including the pink jersey, Cottur, all with the same time as Leoni.

Overall after Stage 5: 1. Cottur, 34:22:44; 2. M. Fazio, at 1:18; 3. Schaer and Ronconi, at 1:34; 5. Jomaux, at 2:02; 6. Carrea, at 2:11; 7. F. Coppi, at 2:58; 8. Leoni, at 3:13; 9. De Santi, at 3:18; 10. Biagioni, at 3:25; 11. Martini and Logli, at 3:43; 13. Bartali, at 3:58.

Stage 6, Naples-Rome
1. Mario Ricci, 233km in 7:07:50 (average 32.676 kph, bonus 1:00); 2. Frosini (bonus 0:30); 3. Pasotti (bonus 0:15); 4. Vincenzo Rossello; 5. Schaer; 6. Busancano, all s.t.; 7. Cerami, at 0:08; 8. Dubuisson, s.t.; 9. Leoni, at 0:30; 10. Conte; 11. Bartali; then several more racers, all with the same time as Leoni.

Overall after Stage 6: 1. Cottur, 41:31:04; 2. Schaer, at 1:04; 3. M. Fazio, at 1:18; 4. Ronconi, at 1:34; 5. Jomaux, at 2:02; 6. Carrea, at 2:11; 7. F. Coppi, at 2:58; 8. Leoni, at 3:13; 9. Biagioni, at 3:23; 10. De Santi, at 3:33; 11. Martini and Logli, at 3:43; 13. Bartali, at 3:58.

Stage 7, Rome-Pesaro
1. Leoni, 298km in 8:01:06 (average 37.101 kph, bonus 1:00); 2. L. Maggini, at 0:30 (bonus 0:30); 3. Pasotti, at 0:34 (bonus 0:15); 4. Bevilacqua, s.t.; 5. Vincenzo Rossello, at 0:49; 6. Logli, at 1:00; 7. Valeriano Zanazzi; 8. tied, with the same time as Logli, Cerami, Ronconi (bonus 0:15), Vicini, M. Fazio, Cecchi, Rossi, Tonini, Castellucci, Franchi; 17. Casola, at 2:44; 18. Bartali; 19. Schaer; 20. Doni; 21. Pezzi; 22. Fornara; 23. Biagioni; 24. Coppini; 25. tied, with the same time as Casola, Astrua, Bresci, Brignole, Corrieri, Cottur, F. Coppi, Fondelli, Fumagalli, Goldschmidt, Jomaux, Lambertini, Martini, Vittorio Magni, Milano, Pedroni, Simonini.

Overall after Stage 7: 1. M. Fazio, 49:34:28; 2. Ronconi, at 0:01; 3. Cottur, at 0:26; 4. Leoni, at 0:55; 5. Schaer, at 1:30; 6. Logli, at 2:25; 7. Jomaux, at 2:28; 8. F. Coppi, at 3:24; 9. Biagioni, at 3:49; 10. Martini, at 4:09; 11. Bartali, at 4:24.

Stage 8, Pesaro-Venice
1. Casola, 273km in 8:19:07 (average 32.817 kph, bonus 1:00); 2. Leoni, at half a length (bonus 0:30); 3. Ricci, s.t. (bonus 0:15); 4. Logli; 5. Conte; 6. tied, all with the same time as Casola, 66 other racers including Bartali, Coppi, Cottur, Fazio, Ronconi.

Overall after Stage 8: 1. M. Fazio, 57:53:35; 2. Ronconi, at 0:01; 3. Leoni, at 0:10; 4. Cottur, at 0:26; 5. Schaer, at 1:30; 6. Logli, at 2:25; 7. Jomaux, at 2:28; 8. Coppi, at 3:24; 9. Biagioni, at 3.49; 10. Martini, at 4:09; 11. Bartali, at 4:24.

Stage 9, Venice-Udine
1. Leoni, 249km in 7:01:20 (average 36.028 kph, bonus 1:00); 2. Pasotti (bonus 0:30); 3. Pezzi (bonus 0:15); 4. Tonini; 5. Doni; 6. Biagioni; 7. Frosini; 8. Castellucci, all s.t.; 9. Ronconi, at 2:53; 10. Schaer; 11. M. Fazio, both s.t.; 12. Bevilacqua, at 4:27; 13. Conte (bonus 0:15); 14. Seghezzi; 15. Jomaux; 16. Soldani; 17. Bartali; 18. Paolieri; 19. Simonini; 20. Missine; 21. F. Coppi, all s.t.; 22, tied, at same time, 50 other riders.

Overall after Stage 9: 1. Leoni, in 64:53:05; 2. Fazio, at 4:43; 3. Ronconi, at 4:44; 4. Biagioni, at 5.39, 5. Schaer, at 0.13, 0. Cottur, at 0.43, 7. Pezzi, at 0.41, 0. Logli, at 0.42, 9. Jomaux, at 0.45, 10. F. Coppi, at 9:41; 11. Martini, at 10:26; 12. Bartali, at 10:41.

Stage 10, Udine-Bassano
1. Corrieri, 154km in 3:45:41 (average 40.942 kph, bonus 1:00); 2. Doni, at 1:14 (bonus 0:30); 3. Fornara, s.t. (bonus 0:15); 4. Leoni, at 2:05; 5. Servadei; 6. Conte; 7. Seghezzi; 8. Paolieri; 9. Frosini; 10. Logli; 11. Tonini; 12. tied, with the same time as Leoni, 50 other racers including Coppi, Bartali, Fazio, Ronconi.

Overall after Stage 9: 1. Leoni, 68:40:51; 2. Fazio, at 4:43; 3. Ronconi, at 4:44; 4. Biagioni, at 5:39; 5. Schaer, at 6:13; 6. Cottur, at 6:43; 7. Pezzi, at 8:41; 8. Logli, at 8:42; 9. Jomaux, at 8:45; 10. F. Coppi, at 9:41; 11. Martini, at 10:26; 12. Bartali, at 10:41.

Stage 11, Bassano-Bolzano
1. F. Coppi, 237km in 8:13:35 (average 28.809 kph, bonus 3:30); 2. Leoni, at 6:58 (bonus 1:15); 3. Bartali (bonus 1:45); 4. Astrua, both s.t. (bonus 0:15); 5. Vittorio Rossello, at 12:37; 6. Cottur, s.t.; 7. Carrea, at 14:43; 8. Martini, at 15:23; 9. Jomaux, at 15:25; 10. Logli, at 16:18.

Mountains Grand Prix
Passo Rolle: 1. Bartali (bonus 1:00); 2. Coppi, 10 meters behind (bonus 0:30); 3. Astrua (bonus 0:15).
Passo Pordoi: 1. Coppi (bonus 1:00); 2. Leoni, at 3:25 (bonus 0:30); 3. Pasotti (bonus 0:15).
Passo Gardena: 1. Coppi (bonus 1:00); 2. Bartali, at 6:40 (bonus 0:30); 3. Leoni, at 8:03 (bonus 0:15).

Overall after Stage 11: 1. Leoni, 77:00:09; 2. Coppi, at 0:28; 3. Bartali, at 10:11; 4. Cottur, at 13:47; 5. Astrua, at 14:39; 6. Fazio, at 16:30; 7. Ronconi, at 16:31.

Stage 12, Bolzano-Modena
1. Conte, 253km in 7:21:00 (average 34.421 kph, bonus 1:00); 2. Bevilacqua, a half wheel behind (bonus 0:30); 3. Seghezzi (bonus 0:15); 4. Logli; 5. Drei; 6. Barducci; 7. Tonini; 8. Pezzi; 9. Carrea, all s.t.; 10. Leoni, at 4:06; 11. Pedroni; 12. Pasquetti; 13. Soldani; 14. Pasotti; 15. Frosini; 16. tied, the peloton, including Bartali, Coppi, Cottur, all with the same time as Leoni.

Overall after Stage 12: 1. Leoni in 84:25:20; 2. Coppi, at 0:43; 3. Bartali, at 10:26; 4. Cottur, at 14:02; 5. Astrua, at 14:54; 6. Logli, at 15:06; 7. M. Fazio, at 16:45; 8. Ronconi, at 16:46; 9. Biagioni, at 17:41; 10. Schaer, at 18:15.

Stage 13, Modena-Montecatini
1. Leoni, 160km in 5:24:00 (average 31.578 kph, bonus 1:00); 2. Coppi (bonus 0:30); 3. Martini (bonus 0:15); 4. Bartali; 5. Logli; 6. Cottur; 7. Bresci; 8. Soldani; 9. tied, all with the same time as Leoni, Franchi, Rossi, Volpi, Goldschmidt, Pasquini. Fazio, Ronconi, Cecchi.

Mountains Grand Prix
Abetone: 1. Pasotti (bonus 1:00); 2. Bartali (bonus 0:30); 3. Coppi (bonus 0:15); 4. Astrua; 5. V. Magni.
Overall: 1. Coppi, 22pts; 2. Bartali. 16pts; 3. Pasotti, 11pts.

Overall after Stage 13: 1. Leoni, 89:48:20; 2. Coppi, at 0:58; 3. Bartali, at 10:56; 4. Cottur, at 15:02; 5. Logli, at 16:06; 6. Astrua, at 16:20; 7. Fazio, at 17:45; 8. Ronconi, at 17:46; 9. Martini, at 20:26; 10. Schaer, at 21:46.

Stage 14, Montecatini-Genoa
1. Vincenzo Rossello, 228km in 6:35:40 (average 34.573 kph, bonus 1:00); 2. Pedroni, at one bike length (bonus 0:30); 3. Vittorio Rossello, at 0:06 (bonus 0:15); 4. Pezzi, at 2:02; 5. Leoni; 6. Bartali; 7. Ricci; 8. Seghezzi; 9. Logli; 10. Coppi, and all the others, with the same time as Pezzi.

Mountains Grand Prix:
Bracco: 1. Pasotti (bonus 1:00); 2. Logli, at 100 meters (bonus 0:30); 3. Bartali (bonus 0:15); 4. Coppi; 5. Astrua.

Overall after Stage 14: 1. Leoni, 96:06:02; 2. Coppi, at 0:58; 3. Bartali, at 10:41; 4. Logli, at 14:36; 5. Cottur, at 15:02; 6. Astrua, at 16:51; 7. Ronconi, at 17:46; 8. Fazio, at 19:07; 9. Martini, at 20:26; 10. Schaer, at 21:40.

Stage 15, Genoa-San Remo
1. L. Maggini, 136km in 3:50:14 (35.442 kph, bonus 1:00); 2. Soldani (bonus 0:30); 3. Seghezzi (bonus 0:15); 4. Drei; 5. Pasotti; 6. Bevilacqua; 7. Tonini; 8. Rossi; 9. Pezzi, all s.t.; 10. Serse Coppi, at 0:26; 11. Dubuisson, s.t.; 12. Conte, at 0:39; 13. Leoni; 14. Servadei; 15. Brasola, and a group including Coppi, Bartali and Astrua, all s.t.

Overall after Stage 15: 1. Leoni, 99:56:55; 2. Coppi, at 0:58; 3. Bartali, at 10:41; 4. Logli, at 14:36; 5. Cottur, at 15:02; 6. Astrua, at 16:51; 7. Ronconi, at 17:46; 8. Fazio, at 19:07; 9. Martini, at 20:26; 10. Schaer, at 21:20.

Stage 16, San Remo-Cuneo
1. Conte, 190km in 5:45:53 (average 32.959 kph, bonus 1:00); 2. Ricci (bonus 0:30); 3. Tonini (bonus 0:15); 4. Maggini; 5. Pezzi; 6. Brasola; 7. Vittorio Rossello; 8. Dubuisson; 9. Jomaux; 10. Fornara; 11. Pinarello; 12. Serse Coppi, all s.t.; 13. Soldani, at 0:59; 14. Zuccotti; 15. Seghezzi; 16. Logli; 17. Doni; 18. Frosini; 19. Malabrocca; 20. Paolieri, all s.t.

Mountains Grand Prix:
Nava: 1. Vittorio Rossello (bonus 1:00); 2. Bartali, at 0:08 (bonus 0:30);; 3. Coppi, on his wheel (bonus 0:15).

Overall after Stage 16: 1. Leoni, 105:43:47; 2. Coppi, at 0:43; 3. Bartali, at 10:11; 4. Logli, at 14:36; 5. Cottur, at 15:02; 6. Astrua, at 16:51; 7. Ronconi, at 17:46; 8. Fazio, at 19:07; 9. Martini, at 20:26; 10. Schaer, at 22:10.

Stage 17, Cuneo-Pinerolo
1. Coppi, 254km in 9:19:55 (average 27.218 kph, bonus 1:00); 2. Bartali, at 11:52 (bonus 0:30); 3. Martini, at 19:14 (bonus 0:15); 4. Cottur; 5. Bresci; 6. Astrua, all s.t.; 7. Biagioni, at 22:37; 8. Leoni; 9. Drei; 10. Rossi, all s.t.; 11, tied, six others, at s.t.

Mountains Grand Prix:
Col de Vars: 1. Coppi (bonus 1:00); 2. Bartali, at 4:29 (bonus 0:30); 3. Volpi, at 4:31 (bonus 0:15); 4. Jomaux; 5. Astrua.
Col d'Izoard: 1. Coppi (bonus 1:00); 2. Bartali, at 6:54 (bonus 0:30); 3. Jomaux, at 10:41 (bonus 0:15); 4. Astrua; 5. Pasquini.
Col du Montgenèvre: 1. Coppi (bonus 0:15); 2. Bartali, at 6:46 (bonus 0:30); 3. Martini, at 17:40 (bonus 0:15); 4. Astrua; 5. Bresci.
Overall: 1. Coppi, 45pts; 2. Bartali, 35pts; 3. Pasotti, 19pts; 4. Astrua, 13pts.

Overall after Stage 17: 1. Coppi, 115:00:25; 2. Bartali, at 23:20; 3. Leoni, at 25:54; 4. Cottur, at 37:33; 5. Astrua, at 39:22; 6. Martini, at 42:27; 7. Bresci, at 45:38; 8. Biagioni, at 50:21; 9. Logli, at 54:24; 10. Fazio, at 58:55.

Stage 18, Pinerolo-Turin Time Trial
1. Bevilacqua, 65km in 1:32:03 (average 42.368 kph, bonus 1:00); 2. Corrieri, 1:33:35 (bonus 0:30); 3. De Santi, 1:33:36 (bonus 0:15); 4. Coppi, 1:34:11; 5. Astrua, 1:34:24; 6. Cottur, 1:34:50; 7. Ausenda, 1:34:52; 8. Bartali, 1:35:23; 9. Rossi, 1:35:35; 10. Logli, 1:36:31.

Overall after Stage 18: 1. Coppi, 116:34:36; 2. Bartali, at 24:32; 3. Cottur, at 38:12; 4. Leoni, at 38:45; 5. Astrua, at 39:35; 6. Martini, at 48:48; 7. Bresci, at 48:59; 8. Biagioni, at 52:55; 9. Logli, at 56:44; 10. Pedroni, at 1:01:55.

Stage 19, Turin-Milan
1. Corrieri, 262km in 8:50:29 (average 30.141 kph); 2. Ricci; 3. Coppi; 4. Tonini; 5. Brasola; 6. Frosini; 7. Pasotti, all s.t.; 8. tied, a group of 50 or so riders, at s.t.

Mountains Grand Prix:
Madonna del Ghisallo: 1. Bartali (bonus 1:00); 2. Pasotti (bonus 0:30); 3. Martini (bonus 0:15).
Final Overall: 1. Coppi, 46pts; 2. Bartali, 41pts; 3. Pasotti, 23pts; 4. Astrua, 14pts; 5. Jomaux, 12pts.

Final overall: 1. Fausto Coppi, 125:25:50; 2. Bartali, at 23:47; 3. Cottur, at 38:27; 4. Leoni, at 39:01; 5. Astrua, at 39:50; 6. Martini, at 48:48; 7. Bresci, at 49:14; 8. Biagioni, at 53:14; 9. Logli, at 56:59; 10. Pedroni, at 1:02:10; 11. Fazio, at 1:06:10; 12. Maggini, at 1:12:38; 13. Schaer, at 1:15:39.

65 finishers

Independents final classification: 1. Astrua; 2. Biagioni; 3. Pedroni; 4. Mario Fazio; 5. Simonini.

BIBLIOGRAPHY

Collected works
PROSE AND POETRY

Buzzati, Dino. Barnabo delle montagne (Barnabo of the Mountains), novel, Treves-Treccani-Tumminelli, Milan-Rome, 1933.

Bestiario (Bestiary), Milan: Mondadori, 1991.

Congedo a ciglio asciutto di Buzzati (Buzzati's Dry-eyed Farewell), unpublished works, ed. Guido Piovene, "Il Giornale," October 30, 1974.

Cronache terrestri (World reports), News service, ed. Domenico Porzio, Milan: Mondadori, 1972.

Dino Buzzati al Giro d'Italia (Dino Buzzati at the Giro d'Italia), ed. Claudio Marabini, Milan: Mondadori, 1981.

Due Poemetti (Two little poems), poetry, Vicenza: Neri Pozza, 1967.

Egregio signore, siamo spiacenti di... (Dear sir, we regret to...), illustrated by Siné, Milano: Elmo, 1960; with the title "Siamo spiacenti di...," Milan: Mondadori, 1975.

Esperimento di magia (Occult Experience), short stories, Padua: Rebellato, 1958.

Il buttafuoco (The Flame-thrower), Mondadori, Milan, 1992.

Il capitano Pic e altre poesie (Captain Pic and other poems), Vicenza: Neri Pozza, 1965.

Il colombre (The Dove), short stories, Milan: Mondadori, 1966.

Il crollo della Baliverna (The Collapse of the Baliverna), short stories, Milan: Mondadori, 1957.

Il deserto dei Tartari (The Desert of the Tartars), novel, Milan: Rizzoli, 1940.

Il grande ritratto (The Big Picture), novel, Milan: Mondadori, 1960.

Il libro delle pipe (All about Pipes), with G. Ramazotti, Milan: Antonioli, 1945.

Il meglio dei racconti (The Best Short Stories), ed. Federico Roncoroni, Milan: Mondadori, 1990.

Il reggimento parte all'alba (The Regiment Leaves at Dawn), with notes by I. Montanelli and G. Piovene, Milan: Frassinelli, 1985.

Il segreto del Bosco Vecchio (The Secret of the Old Forest), novel, Milan-Rome: Treves-Treccani- Tumminelli, 1935; single volume with Barnabo of the Mountains, Milan: Garzanti, 1957.

I miracoli di Val Morel (The Val Morel Miracles), Milan: Garzanti, 1971.

I misteri d'Italia (Italy's Mysteries), Milan: Mondadori, 1978.

In quel preciso momento (At that precise moment), notes, comments and short stories, Vicenza: Neri Pozza, 1950.

I sette messaggeri (The Seven Messengers), short stories, Milan: Mondadori, 1942.

La boutique del mistero (The Mystery Boutique), short stories, Milan: Mondadori, 1968.

La famosa invasione degli orsi in Sicilia (The Bears' Famous Invasion of Sicily), ill. children's book, Milan: Rizzoli, 1945.

Le montagne di vetro (The Glass Mountains), ed. Enrico Camanni, Turin: Vivalda, 1990.

Le notti difficili (The difficult Nights), Milan: Mondadori, 1971.

Le storie dipinte (The Painted Stories), ed. Mario Oriani and Adriano Ravegnani, Milan: All'insegna dei Re Magi, 1958.

Lettere a Brambilla (Letters to Brambilla), ed. Luciano Simonelli, Novara: De Agostini, 1985.

Lo strano Natale di Mr. Scrooge e altre storie (Mr. Scrooge's Strange Christmas and other stories), ed. Domenico Porzio, Milan: Mondadori, 1990.

Paura alla Scala (Fear at La Scala), short stories, Milan: Mondadori, 1949.

Poema a fumetti (Comic-strip Poem), Milan: Mondadori, 1969.

Prefazione a R, James, Cuori strappati (Foreword to R, James, Broken Hearts, Milan: Bompiani, 1967.

Prefazione a Tarzan delle scimmie (Foreword to Tarzan of the Apes), Florence: Giunti, 1971.

Prefazione a W. Disney, Vita e dollari di Paperon de Paperoni (Foreword to W. Disney, Donald Duck's Life and Money), Milan: Mondadori, 1968.

Romanzi e racconti (Novels and Short Stories), ed. Giuliano Gramigna, Milan: Mondadori, 1975.

Scusi da che parte per Piazza Duomo? introduzione in versi (Excuse me, which way to Piazza Duomo?, introduction in verse), Milan: Alfieri, 1965.

Sessanta racconti (Sixty Short Stories), from previously published collections, including unpublished and rare items, Milan: Mondadori,1958.

Teatro (Theater), ed. Guido Bonino, Milan: Mondadori, 1980.

Tre colpi alla porta, poema satirico (Three Knocks on the Door, a satirical poem), "Il caffé," n.5, 1965.

Un amore (A Love Affair), novel, Milan: Mondadori, 1975.

180 racconti (180 Short Stories), ed. Carlo Della Corte, Milan-Rome-Naples: Theoria, 1984.

PLAYS

Piccola passeggiata (A Little Walk), printed text not found, Rome, 1946.

La rivolta contro i poveri (The Rebellion Against the Poor), "Film notebooks," Rome, 1946.

Un caso clinico (A Clinical Case), Milan: Mondadori, 1953.

Drammatica fine di un musicista (Dramatic End of a Musician), "Corrier d'Informazione," November 3-4, 1955.

Sola in casa (Alone at Home), "L'Illustrazione italiana," May 1958.

Una ragazza arrivó (A Girl Arrived), Milan: Bietti, 1958.

L'orologio (The Clock), unpublished, 1959.

Le finestre (The Windows), "Corriere d'Informazione," June 3-4, 1959.

Un verme al ministero (A Worm at the Ministry), "Il dramma," April 1960.

Il mantello (The Cape), "Il dramma," June, 1960.

I suggeritori (The Prompters), "Documento Moda 1960," 1960.

L'Uomo che andó in America (The Man Who Went to America), "Il dramma," June 1962.

La colonna infame (The Infamous Column), "Il dramma," December 1962.

Spogliarello (Striptease), unpublished, 1964.

La fine del borghese (The End of the Middle Class), Milano: Bietti, 1968.

LIBRETTI

Procedura penale (Criminal Procedure), Milan: Ricordi, 1959.

Ferrovia sopraelevata (Elevated Railway), Milan: Ferriani, 1960.

Il mantello (The Cape), Milan: Ricordi, 1960.

Battono alla porta (Someone is Knocking at the Door), Milan: Suvini-Zerboni, 1963.

Era probito (It was forbidden), Milan: Ricordi, 1963.